NOTES

Isaiah - 9:6-7
Rule w/ fairness & justice.

John 1: 1-14
"Unfailing love & faithfulness"

John 12: 24-25
Matthew: 20:28

What am I willing to
Sacrifice for others?

The only perfect man
takes the punishment for
imperfect people.

1 John 4:10

CHRIST'S CHURCH
DAILY LIFE JOURNAL SCRIPTURE
S.O.A.P

MARCH 4. JUDGES 2	**MARCH 7.** JUDGES 5	**MARCH 11.** JUDGES 8
MARCH 5. JUDGES 3	**MARCH 8.** JUDGES 6	**MARCH 12.** JUDGES 9
MARCH 6. JUDGES 4	**MARCH 9.** JUDGES 7	**MARCH 13.** JUDGES 10

THURSDAY NIGHTS AT CC MANDARIN CAMPUS
THURSDAYS AT 6:30PM, MANDARIN CAMPUS

Can't make it to church on Sunday? No worries, we've got you covered! Join us for church on Thursday nights at the CC Mandarin Campus. It's identical to Sunday and offers an exciting time of worship and community. You can also enjoy a free bite of something good to eat! www.Christs.Church/Thursday

EMERGENCE
MONDAY NIGHTS, MANDARIN CAMPUS

We all participate in worship, but some of us have a particular passion for leading others in worship through music and tech. **Emergence School of Worship** gives you space to explore and develop your gifts and equips you as a worship leader, artist and technician. **Emergence Kids** develops kids' passion for worship and expands their abilities in music and tech. Register at www.EmergenceWorship.com

HOLY LAND TOUR 2019

Walking on ground that Jesus walked and touching rocks He might have sat on is a thrilling experience for many believers. A trip to the Holy Land can give you a new understanding of Christian history and the life of Jesus. Pastor Jason Cullum will take you to places where Jesus walked, lived, and taught, where He was crucified and raised from the dead. Boat on the Sea of Galilee, take communion at the Garden Tomb, and be baptized in the Jordan River. Contact Jennifer Nelson (904) 493-5466, JenniferN@Christs.Church or visit www.Christs.Church/HolyLand for additional details.

SHARING TREE MANDARIN REGISTRATION

Children learn and grow so much in their early years. Let Sharing Tree Preschool partner with you to cultivate your child's love for learning and set the stage for their future success. Sharing Tree is enrolling now for the 2019/2020 school year. Visit www.Christs.Church/SharingTree or call 904-260-2015.

 HEARING HELP AVAILABLE in the Worship Center at the Mandarin Campus

YOUR GENEROSITY MAKES A DIFFERENCE!

online	on-site	text
WEB | APP	KIOSKS | GIVING BOXES	TEXT TO GIVE
Automate your giving online. www.Christs.Church/Giving	Located outside the Worship Center these enable you to give onsite if you prefer.	Text "CCGIVE" to 1-206-859-9405

There's a real hunger for knowledge about what it means to be a man. Men are responding in profound ways to the gospel through the Act Like Men conferences. James MacDonald continues that track in this book by providing a biblical framework on how to align the head and heart on God's plan.

MATT CHANDLER
Lead pastor of The Village Church, Flower Mound, TX,
author of *The Explicit Gospel*

All around us society is failing at the places where men must succeed. *Act Like Men* is a clear call at a critical hour for men to step up and fulfill the purposes of their Creator. James MacDonald uses the Word of God with urgency and authenticity to call us out as men. I can only pray that we hear and answer this call—the time is now.

DR. JACK GRAHAM
Pastor of Prestonwood Baptist Church, Dallas, TX, author of *A Man of God*

I'm so thankful for Pastor James MacDonald's new book, *Act Like Men*. This message is timely, direct, and full of spiritual truth poised to transform lives. By God's grace, James's words will help you become the man God created you to be.

CRAIG GROESCHEL
Pastor of LifeChurch.tv and author of *FIGHT—Winning the Battles That Matter Most*

What we need are radical, committed men of God who are not afraid to stand up for what is true. My friend James MacDonald is such a man. And in this powerful new resource, he calls us and shows us how to be that kind of man.

GREG LAURIE
Senior pastor, Harvest Christian Fellowship, Riverside, CA, founder of Harvest Crusades

It isn't easy for a man to be honest with other men. We can be funny, serious, flippant, crude, rude—anything but honest. James shows us in *Act Like Men* why we miss out on the main thing when we won't push through to honesty.

BRYAN LORITTS
Lead pastor of Fellowship Memphis and author of *A Cross-Shaped Gospel: Reconciling Heaven and Earth*

Men, it's time for things to be different. God is calling you to what HE wants you to be. If you're ready to make a change, and you're serious about it, you won't waste another minute before jumping into this study. It could be one of the best decisions you've made in your pursuit of biblical manhood.

ERIC MASON
Founder and pastor of Epiphany Fellowship, Philadelphia, PA,
and author of *Manhood Restored: How the Gospel Makes Men Whole*

40 DAYS TO BIBLICAL MANHOOD

JAMES MACDONALD

MOODY PUBLISHERS
CHICAGO

Published in association with the literary agency of Wolgemuth and Associates, Inc.

Unless otherwise indicated, Scripture quotations are from The Holy Bible, English Standard Version® (ESV®), copyright © 2001 by Crossway, a publishing ministry of Good News Publishers. Used by permission. All rights reserved.

Scripture quotations marked NKJV are taken from the *New King James Version*. Copyright © 1982 by Thomas Nelson, Inc. Used by permission. All rights reserved.

Scripture quotations marked HCSB are taken from the *Holman Christian Standard Bible*®, copyright © 1999, 2000, 2002, 2003 by Holman Bible Publishers. Used by permission. Holman Christian Standard Bible®, Holman CSB®, and HCSB® are federally registered trademarks of Holman Bible Publishers.

Scripture quotations marked NASB are taken from the *New American Standard Bible*®, copyright © 1960, 1962, 1963, 1968, 1971, 1972, 1973, 1975, 1977, 1995 by The Lockman Foundation. Used by permission. (www.Lockman.org)

Scripture quotations marked KJV are taken from the King James Version.

Scripture quotations marked NIV are taken from the *Holy Bible, New International Version*®, NIV®. Copyright © 1973, 1978, 1984, 2011 by Biblica, Inc.™ Used by permission of Zondervan. All rights reserved worldwide. www.zondervan.com. The "NIV" and "New International Version" are trademarks registered in the United States Patent and Trademark Office by Biblica, Inc.™

Edited by Neil Wilson and Pam Pugh
Interior Design: Erik M. Peterson
Cover Design: Nate Baron
Cover Image: Lightstock (www.lightstock.com)

Library of Congress Cataloging-in-Publication Data

MacDonald, James, 1960–
Act like men / James MacDonald.
    pages cm
Includes bibliographical references.
ISBN 978-0-8024-5719-6
1. Christian men—Religious life. 2. Men (Christian theology) I. Title.
BV4528.2.M27 2014
248.8'42--dc23
                        2014022192

We hope you enjoy this book from Moody Publishers. Our goal is to provide high-quality, thought-provoking books and products that connect truth to your real needs and challenges. For more information on other books and products written and produced from a biblical perspective, go to www.moodypublishers.com or write to:

Moody Publishers
820 N. LaSalle Boulevard
Chicago, IL 60610

7 9 10 8 6

Printed in the United States of America

TO MY SONS LUKE AND LANDON
AND FIVE (SO FAR) GRANDSONS
CARTER, MONTIE, REID, GRAHAM, AND EZRA
WITH THE PRAYER THAT WE WOULD ALL
"ACT LIKE MEN" ALWAYS.

CONTENTS

Foreword   9

Introduction   11

SECTION 1: *Act Like Men*   23

SECTION 2: *Be Watchful*   73

SECTION 3: *Stand Firm in the Faith*   121

SECTION 4: *Be Strong*   165

SECTION 5: *Let All That You Do Be Done in Love*   215

Act Like Men Book Matrix   264

Notes   266

FOREWORD

EARLY ON IN MY CHURCH planting experiences, I met with a group of men for Bible study. Together, we looked carefully at the qualities of maturity outlined by the apostle Paul in his letters to Timothy and Titus—a twenty-weeks experience that was life changing for all of us. Our goal was to measure up more and more to the fullness of Christ.

As a result, a publishing friend of mine encouraged me to write *The Measure of a Man*. Little did I realize how God was going to use it—even to this day—not because I wrote it but because the qualities of maturity came from the pen of Paul as he wrote by the inspiration of the Holy Spirit.

The basic characteristics of maturity in this book—*Act Like Men*—authored by James MacDonald—also come from the pen of the apostle Paul when he wrote to the Corinthians. It is a succinct and powerful profile for becoming mature in Christ:

> *Be watchful, stand firm in the faith, **act like men**, be strong.*
> *Let all that you do be done in love.* (1 Corinthians 16:13–14)

In many respects, I've watched this book emerge. Though James MacDonald and I had known each other casually, we developed a growing friendship several years ago when he was going through some very deep waters. Though incredibly successful as a senior pastor at Harvest Bible Chapel with an exploding network of affiliated churches and a worldwide broadcast ministry, he was facing serious criticisms in his own church.

Through a series of events, James invited me into his life as a mentor and encourager. Having been down the road many miles as a church planting pastor, I too have been through some tough terrain. Like him, I had made some decisions and statements that resulted in some very painful experiences. I was simply able to share from my own ministry life.

As I reflect on our face-to-face communications, dozens of telephone calls, emails, and texts—I discovered a man who wanted to learn, rebuild bridges that were broken down, and overall make changes in his life and approach to leadership. I discovered a man who sincerely desires to reflect the humility of Jesus Christ in every aspect of his life. Consequently, this book, *Act Like Men*, reflects not only the author's unique ability to communicate God's truth but the way in which God's truth is impacting his own ministry and family.

Let me address this book from two perspectives—personally and pragmatically. First, what makes MacDonald's words very powerful and convicting—beyond speaking God's truth—is his vulnerability in personal matters. His struggles are on display as well as his steps to victory— making his straightforward exhortations authentic and convicting.

Second, this book reflects a pragmatic design that will appeal to men. The chapters are short and pithy. His opening stories and illustrations will grab your attention. His expositions and applications are an easy read! His questions at the end of each chapter will lead you to deeper engagement and are great for group discussion. And his prayers at the end of every chapter reflect the author's own sincere desire and quest to be the man God created him to be. I identify with the spirit and content of these prayers—and I'm confident you will too! They focus on needs in every man's heart and life. Alone, if taken seriously, these prayers could change your life.

DR. GENE A. GETZ
Professor, Pastor, Author
President, Center for Church Renewal
Plano, TX

INTRODUCTION

HEY, DON'T SKIP THE INTRODUCTION!

Most men like to know what they're getting themselves into and what it will take to make the finish line. This overview tells you where we're going in this book, how we'll get there, and how your investment in reading it can make a real and lasting difference in your life. It's a little longer than usual, but I promise the individual chapters/studies will be much shorter than you expect.

"What do you want first, the good news or the bad news?" It's the kind of bumpy start you expect when a tough subject has to be discussed. Typically the nervous person with the hard message to deliver, finding no easy point of access, begins with that common question, "So, what do you want first?" Then they launch with the bad news regardless of your answer, so here goes.

BAD NEWS: MEN ARE IN TROUBLE

Men are in deep trouble with sin. Every statistic says that most men are somewhere between dabbling on the edges of a self-disqualifying and self-destructive sin, *or* actually wading right into it. In fact, the five main areas where men spend their money—electronics, sports, cars, gambling, and alcohol—are all clues to a self-centered perspective. Men are struggling, stumbling, and proving notoriously weak in the face of temptation. The rampant spread of Internet porn is devouring men's souls like a new and deadly form of cancer. Its lure of private pleasure turns out to be a thin veil over the havoc it causes in marriages and public lives. The decay of sin is everywhere. This isn't going anywhere good. Something has to change.

These issues have immediate and long-term impact on those we love most. We're losing our kids. Even when marriages remain unbroken, how many children are growing up without what God designed men as fathers to give? Paternity is a long way from fatherhood. Two-income families may relieve financial pressure, but it doesn't prepare kids for the moral minefield that is waiting to detonate their hopes and dreams.

Men are also in trouble because of their own shallow spirituality. In a 2013 Forbes article entitled *"14 Things Successful People Do on Weekends,"* there isn't even a mention of God. Western world–watered-down church was reshaped to reach men but it bores them like a Saturday afternoon trip to Target. Men want to do something hard. Men want to be challenged to stretch and test the limits of who they are. God designed them that way and church is placating men instead of calling them to something much higher. I won't make that mistake here.

MORE BAD NEWS: MEN DON'T WORK ON THEMSELVES

Most women put forth continual efforts to learn and improve themselves. The biggest category of books is "self-help," and women are the ones forking over the cash to see how they can grow. Guys work on projects; women work on themselves. Guys roof the garage, paint the basement, and fix the kids' bikes; women think about relationships and focus on their families. Yes, of course I know there are exceptions to these broad generalizations. We all know the guy who gets a pedicure and frosts his tips, but most men think that guy is wacky and only talk to him when forced. We also know the woman who swears like a sailor and changes the oil in her own car—but if she's your wife, that says more about you than it does about her. Both cases are simply the exceptions that prove the rule. This is not a book for the 500 men in the world who read *GQ* magazine; or the 250 men debating theology as an end in itself. This is a book for Joe Screwdriver, the regular guy, like you and me (more on Joe in a moment).

SOUL WORK

Soul is not a kind of food or a style of music. It is the seat of man's desire, the place where "wanting" resides. The soul is the nonphysical part of every human being that sets us apart from the animals. Your soul is made up of mind, emotion, and will; it's the place where you think and feel and choose. When your soul is satisfied, you have everything even if you have nothing. And when your soul is not at peace, you have nothing no matter what you have attained or acquired. Soul work is hard work. Failure to extend the effort has us stuffing our demanding souls with all kinds of selfish, superattractive but unsatisfying scraps the Bible calls sin. It cuts a swath of destruction across a man's life like a tornado across a Nebraska cornfield.

So instead of consuming more sex and pursuing more power and other selfish stuff, like we devour popcorn shrimp at a Super Bowl party, we're going to do something stretching here and it will be worth it. Yes, this is your time to turn from those things that have only made you restless and miserable, and to get busy on the role God created you to fulfill—which will bring a joy you never thought possible. First, though, one more piece of bad news.

EVEN MORE BAD NEWS: MEN DON'T READ

If you know anything about men, you know we generally don't read many books or spend a ton of time talking to the few men who do read, and read, and read. Most men consider it a chore to consult the instruction manual about how to assemble something—and would rather build it twice than study something longer than playoff scores. Men are famous for refusing even the two-second step of reading road signs, let alone reading a map (which is more pictures than words and not real reading at all). Book retailers will tell you that most books are read by women, even books for men, and very few books of any kind are written specifically for guys. What would be the point? So here goes crazy me, throwing down where angels fear to tread. I'm writing this book with the wild goal that men who can't remember the last book they opened, and don't plan to read in the future, would take the time to read this.

I want to help real men who are facing real issues and in need of a big-time turnaround. This is not a bit of helpful advice but a total renovation of what you are doing with your life and why. If you're tired of living for sex and sandwiches or something just as silly, you are on the right track. Now for the good news.

GOOD NEWS: KEEP IT SIMPLE, STUPID

Kiss is more than a seventies rock band with hair in their ears and Viagra in their pockets. Kiss has become an acronym for the stupidity of not keeping things as simple as possible. This is especially important for men. The stupid guy isn't the dude who rejects complicated treatises on biblical masculinity and reading theological speculations about the third heaven. The stupid person is the guy who can't put complex truth in a way that everyday men can appreciate it. I hope to avoid that stupidity here.

It has always been instructive to me that the Holy Spirit inspired the apostle Peter to use six verses, 151 English words to describe in detail and illustrate the role of women in marriage (1 Peter 3:1–6). Why then only a single verse (38 English words) to describe a man's responsibility to his wife (1 Peter 3:7)? Answer: Because men like it boiled down, bottom line, give it to me quick and let me get after it. Men also like it direct. Not talking about some other guy but talking to you, the guy holding the book. For that reason I am going to change the "voice" of this book right now. Voice is the position the author takes as he writes. I am not going to write anymore as a third party saying things about men. This is a book about me and you (see the difference?). The content may be upsetting to your sensibilities but you will never have to wonder about my subject or my audience.

"Are you talking to me?" (picture DeNiro with rough New York accent). "You talkin' to me?"

Yes I am. My goal is to talk to you through these pages in a clear, direct, and to-the-point way. You may find some parts tough to take and challenging to apply, but I promise you won't ever wonder what I am talking about. If you get ticked, put the book down and come back to it later. Further, because you shouldn't have to take my word for anything, I am going to base all I write on the Bible. God's Word has been redirecting men's hearts for thousands of years, and we do well to show it some respect and carefully consider its message.

MORE GOOD NEWS: YOU CAN HAVE A FRESH START

I am writing from the perspective of a Christian. The good news of the gospel of Jesus Christ is that God loves sinful men. He did not come to condemn them or to judge them; He came to save men, to rebuild them, to transform them for His purposes. God takes lives that are stuck on sin and selfishness and reboots them. If you picked up this book because you need God to redeem your regrets and restore what sin has stolen from you, this is going to be awesome.

When I was seventeen, God took hold of my life with the message of love and forgiveness that is found in Jesus Christ and He has never let go. If you know and love the Lord or if you are just new to all this, the message remains the same: God loves you; Jesus died to secure your forgiveness; and if you are ready to turn from all patterns of sin and believe in the resurrected Savior, Jesus Christ, for your forgiveness, you can begin again with the assurance that God accepts you and is committed to building you into a new man.

STILL MORE GOOD NEWS: THIS BOOK IS FOR REGULAR GUYS

Allow me to introduce a friend of mine. Joe Screwdriver works a job he is not always crazy about, and never seems to finish his wife's list of house stuff that needs to get fixed, cleaned, or put away. He used to think about doing something grand and becoming someone great, but now he's just glad to be getting by. Joe is married with kids and wants it to last for a ton of good reasons.

MEMO TO SINGLE GUYS

By the way, if you're single or single again, you should read this book, but understand that it's about where you are trying to get to or get back to. I'm not gonna keep writing separate stuff for you like you are okay to stay where you are unless you have a direct word from God Almighty Himself asking you to stay single. I kinda want you single guys to get busy and pick one of the two trillion amazing/available Christian women who are waiting for you to get tired of Call of Duty and porn, or however you have been spinning your wheels. I want you to find a good woman and get serious about building a legacy of Christ-honoring kids and grandkids. Okay?

Now back to Mr. Screwdriver, who loves his family dearly but finds it tough at times to tell them how he feels. He goes to church but doesn't always get much from it and sometimes won't think about God again until next week. Joe prays, but mostly a sentence or two in times of desperation. Joe wants to know God better but wonders why it always seems like work. Joe has enough money to pay the bills and tries not to buy dumb stuff he can't afford, a mistake he never wants to make again. Joe is about getting the job done and would never call himself unhappy, but truthfully, he doesn't have a ton of time to think about such things. Joe is not concerned with fashion, isn't overly punctual or neat, and he's not a fan of fake anything. He can't figure out what the guy with the hair plugs is going for. Joe knows he's just the average guy, the face in the crowd, the forgotten majority. His voice is not heard, his thoughts are not sought out, and his opinions seem totally unheard in the noise of the world's loudmouths who would rather be infamous than anonymous.

If you don't understand men, you might see Joe as complicated, but if you study him, he's actually pretty predictable. Joe knows what he knows and is a stand-up, straight-ahead guy. I wrote my doctoral thesis to help Joe be more open about the things he struggles with, and I started a church in a warehouse because Joe doesn't need fluff or fancy. I think about Joe when I have a sermon to prepare, but this is the first time I have ever written a whole book with Joe in mind and I am excited about the challenge. I love this guy. Joe Screwdriver is the sum total of all the men I have ever known. He is in fact "everyman" because he doesn't represent the few things that make us different. Joe Screwdriver epitomizes the many, many things that make you and me so similar as men.

Does this sound familiar? Joe Screwdriver gets angry about injustice, especially toward women and children. He likes sports but doesn't live for them. He loves a close game, especially if the underdog pulls it out in overtime, because Joe feels like regular folk could use a leg up in this world. Right now, Joe is wondering if I will ever stop babbling and cut to the chase with some actual help. Yes I will, Joe, right now.

HOW TO GET THE MOST FROM *ACT LIKE MEN*

TWO MAIN BIBLE VERSES OUTLINE THIS BOOK

I will use a lot of Bible verses sprinkled throughout the chapters, but don't be overwhelmed. The book is really about two main Bible verses I want you to learn. At the end of Paul's first letter to the Corinthians, he exhorts believers to take hold of what they long for and what God created them to be and experience. In 1 Thessalonians 2:7 Paul challenges all Christians to demonstrate the tenderness best illustrated in a nursing mother with her children. While that sensitive care is natural to a mother, it is commanded of us all. In the same way, Paul in 1 Corinthians 16:13–14, exhorts all believers to reflect the strengths that are relative to masculinity. While these characteristics are also to be seen in each of us, they should come most naturally and are needed most urgently in men. The purpose of this book is to call men to lead the way in exhibiting these characteristics that reflect God's creative intent for masculinity.

"Be watchful, stand firm in the faith, act like men, be strong. Let all that you do be done in love" (1 Corinthians 16:13–14).

Five imperatives, simple direct commands that when rightly understood don't leave room to wiggle. In these five imperatives I see a wonderful summary of what God intends for you and me. The middle exhortation, "act like men," is the defining center around which the other four exhortations gather, so we will handle it first. "Act like men" is the hub, if you will, of the wheel that biblical masculinity rolls around. Put the five together and they form a fantastic game plan for men seeking clear direction on how to order their priorities in a God-honoring, soul-satisfying way. And because it is directed to men, God's instruction comes to us the way men want it: condensed and straight to the point!

- Assertion #1—act like men; the *quality* imperative the other four rally around
- Assertion #2—be watchful; an imperative about *urgency* and getting after what matters most of all
- Assertion #3—stand firm; the urgency imperative derails if we don't have *clarity*
- Assertion #4—be strong; the imperative of *authenticity* and freedom from pretense
- Assertion #5—all done in love; the final imperative of lasting, satisfying *community that fuels the other four*

Okay, got it? Five sections, one about each biblical imperative and how total obedience to it can fulfill what God made us as men to experience.

40 STUDIES IN ALL

Long chapters tend to bore men and frustrate them when they can't sit long enough to plow through one. For that reason, each of the five sections out of our theme verse of 1 Corinthians 16:13–14 will be examined briefly from eight common angles. See the chart on page 264.

Each section will cover:

1. The biblical imperative, what it means and what it looks like in our lives
2. The single word that best defines what the imperative means and how to experience it
3. An Old Testament example, a man who refused this imperative and suffered the consequences
4. The way the apostle Paul exemplified this imperative and how you can too

5. The satanic lie men believe that keeps us from embracing this imperative
6. How God the Father perfects that imperative
7. How Jesus Christ personifies that imperative
8. How the Holy Spirit empowers that imperative

Okay, got it. Eight studies about each of the five imperatives for a total of forty studies.

WHY STUDY BIBLICAL MEN?

Some of the guys in the Bible are "real characters," if you know what I mean. They went through a lot of messy stuff to get to the place where they knew they needed God more than anyone or anything. If you are not there yet, that's okay. These men are mentioned in God's Word for a reason. They are not glossy or retouched photos that mask a darker reality. Don't think that we can't relate to these biblical men because centuries separate us from them. The stark revelation of their struggles and what God taught them reveal that the way men have changed through the centuries is meaningless compared to the ways we have stayed the same. We are gonna learn from a Bible man's mistakes in every chapter as well as from the example of Paul, and finally from the God-man Jesus Christ.

WHY THE PERSONAL STORIES?

One of the biggest hindrances to relationship among men is our tendency to hold things inside. We hide and cover and close ourselves off to the kind of openness that causes male friendships to flourish and faith in God to grow. You may be fearful of making yourself known. Possibly you are fearful, or have been hurt, or only ever learned to bottle up what you experience. Amazing things happen when men drop their guard and get honest with each other, and I am going to take the difficult step of going first. In almost every study, I am going to use personal illustrations. More by far than in any of the other books I have written. I am going to be pretty open about lessons I have learned, mistakes I have made, situations I have gotten myself into, etc. It's not that I think my life is interesting, and I would rather keep it private in many ways. But my prayer is that through opening up about hard stuff I have had to learn, you will feel like you have permission to do the same, because that's when the change really begins to happen. It would be incredible if you read this book slowly and discussed it with other men as you move through it. That will make all the difference.

QUESTIONS FOR REFLECTION

You will notice a space to write some things down. Keep this book in a private place so you won't fear others reading what you write. If you can't be sure, use a separate journal. I will be encouraging you to get another man you respect to read this book at the same time. Possibly you can meet to discuss your answers. The important purpose of the questions is to open up your mind to what you have been reading, ensure you understand it, and begin thinking about the changes needed to see that soul-craving more fully satisfied in your life. The value of doing these studies alongside another guy is that it will increase the probability of getting through the process.

PRAYERS TO PRAY

Each chapter ends with a targeted prayer to pray. Don't skip these. They are not formulaic prayers but requests and confessions I have made for you and for myself in writing this book and launching the Act Like Men conferences. If you humble yourself before God, even kneel down and pray out loud, alone, where no one can hear you, something very powerful will begin to happen. You will sense God's presence with you and His favor upon your strong and growing desire to experience the very purposes for which He made you.

In fact, let's stop to pray right now.

INTRODUCTION

Father in heaven,
My longing to be the man You have created me to be is
exceeded only by my acute awareness that I am not yet that
man. Thank You for leading me to the place where I am now
holding a plan to get to a better place. Please forgive me for the
times I have failed to act like a man and for the grief that has
caused others who count on me. Birth in my heart this moment
a focused hope that You have something better in store for
me and those I love. Thank You for the grace that allows me to
change. I pray for the strength to seize this opportunity with my
whole heart. In Jesus' name I pray, amen.

**OKAY, TURN THE PAGE AND
LET'S GET INTO SECTION #1.**

1

ACTING LIKE MEN

Be watchful, stand firm in the faith, act like men, be strong. Let all that you do be done in love.[1]

I WAS PRETTY EXCITED WHEN I walked into the diner and saw a table full of good ol' boys hungrily forking their breakfasts. Truckers, retired farmers, and guys with military insignia on their baseball caps made up the group. These dudes were no-nonsense to be sure and looked up pretty suspiciously as I approached their table.

Our church has a 650-acre camp in Croton, Michigan, and I love to go there when I'm working on a writing project. Croton is located in Newaygo County, a mostly woods, lakes, and small towns area of Michigan. What is lost in bling and bright lights is more than made up for in "real as it gets," straight-shooting authenticity. The particular diner I love to hang out in has no name but the sign says "good food," and it isn't a lie. The place gets pretty packed, overflowing with regular folk who want fresh food for a fair price.

Arriving at the crowded table, I sensed the men stiffen up and wondered if I had made a mistake. "Hey, you guys have a second to answer a question for me?" Everyone froze. "I'm working on a book," I continued. "I recognize a table full of good ol' boys when I see one and I want to know what you think it means to 'act like a man.'"

The first guy to break the silence objected gruffly to my use of the term "old." I scratched my beard and said, "It takes one to know one." Everyone laughed, the tension broke, and they began to eagerly answer my question.

"Acting like a man means doing what you say you're gonna do," the first guy offered.

"It means not doing anything under the table when you are making a deal," another added.

"Keeping your word," a man they called the "Mayor" declared.

"And not making any excuses," added the first man, jumping back in.

"Yes." They all seemed to chime in at that. "Nothing worse than a man who makes excuses, blames others, and refuses responsibility for his own actions." No doubt there were real experiences that underlined the worthlessness of excuse makers for these men.

You can learn a lot from regular folk who are too immersed in life's realities to posture for anyone. Every one of those guys is a Joe Screwdriver of sorts, and I renewed my determination to write a book that could connect with good men like them.

The Bible asserts that the words it contains are God's words and they are **"living and active."**[2] I know this is true because I have been studying the Bible for more than three decades but I never open it without finding stuff I didn't see before, even in places I have studied in depth. That's why I shouldn't have been surprised when a recent journey through 1 Corinthians yielded an observation that had evaded me these many years. How could I have missed Paul's exhortation in 1 Corinthians 16:13 to **"act like men"**? I have witnessed the consequences for many men who have refused this exhortation by their practice, and to my shame I have at times failed to meet this standard myself. In what seemed like my very first reading, the command hit me like a sledgehammer. I wrote the phrase down and began to pray that God would advance my understanding of what it really means to act like a man.

Over a period of weeks and then months, I went back to this phrase again and again. Of course Paul has all believers in mind with his five imperatives; however, it appears that these specific aspects of biblical maturity were best illustrated as expressions of masculinity. I like what Kistemaker states, "Like a general in the army of the Lord, Paul gives short orders in rapid succession and expects his people to put his commands into practice."[3] Clear, direct, succinct, just the way men like it, and while applicable to all, for the purposes of our study we will apply to men what Paul seems to indicate should come naturally to men. The power of these phrases is in their simplicity, and the more I have reflected on them, the more impactful they have become. "Act like men" means a lot of profound things that I hope to share as this book unfolds, but before it reveals anything super deep and insightful, it has to mean the following basics. Because it's just you and me communicating here, let's make Paul's plural into singular: Act like a man!

ACT LIKE A MAN MEANS DON'T ACT LIKE A WOMAN

Obvious, right? I have been happily married for more than thirty years and I have no problem acknowledging that I am a big fan of women in general and my wife, Kathy, specifically. I enjoy some days away with the boys, such as our Idaho bear hunt coming up in a few weeks, but I am always happy to get back to my wife, daughter, and two daughters-in-law. If you have read Genesis, the first book in the Bible, then you might remember that Adam, the first guy, was only around for about ten minutes before God declared, **"It is not good that the man should be alone."**[4] Who knows what trouble this guy was already into, but God was not going to let it continue and provided woman to be **"a helper fit for him."**[5] I think we would all agree that men and women fit together beautifully in every way. Not just physically but emotionally, relationally, and spiritually. One man with one woman for a lifetime is God's plan. Men and women are designed by their Creator to complement and complete, not compete with one another. Each is to become more because of the other than they could ever become alone. That has certainly been true in my life because of Kathy.

I know we live in a world where distinction based on gender is frowned upon but that doesn't alter reality one bit. Men and women are equal under God in every way, but they are not the same. It is possible to make some general observations based on gender. For example, you may have noticed that your woman has a different emotional makeup than you. She is scared by things you don't even notice, like driving with your knee while you hold a coffee and answer the phone, or walking down a dark alley late at night. She is touched by things that may seem silly to you, like a romantic scene in a movie or a person in need who might make you more suspicious.

Proverbs 18:22 says, **"He who finds a wife finds a good thing."** And just like every man needs a good woman, women need men. Most of all they need their man to be a source of strength, stability, and leadership. The major decisions and responsibilities of your home are on you, not your wife. They're your call. Listen to her, learn from her, but don't fail to lead her. Not many things are sadder than a passive man acting more like a woman while his wife is allowed to dominate and usurp the role God has called him to fulfill. It's on you to make sure that doesn't happen, so step up and lead. Lead with love, service, and tenderness to be sure, but act like a man and lead.

Men are made to provide security for their wives. Men are designed to cover women with their strength, offering the protection and security God made them to need. As men we reap the benefits of our wives' emotional tenderness, and we have to make sure we are reciprocating with the strength they need. Sadly though, how many families do you know where the husband is counting on the wife to lead and in some cases even to be the main provider? There are a ton of acceptable divisions of labor that can work in a home, but none where you are not leading. It doesn't matter if she cuts the lawn and you cut the vegetables; it just matters that you lead. Failing to lead is failing to act like a man.

I just checked with my wife and she said it was okay for me to say this.

ACT LIKE A MAN MEANS DON'T ACT LIKE AN ANIMAL

Across the spectrum from the passive man who abdicates his God-given role as leader is the dominant, hypermacho pseudo man, who doesn't love his wife selflessly as Christ commands. Instead he expects to be served and barks selfishly whenever he feels he is not the obvious priority.

Years ago we were honored to welcome a famous special guest into our home. Every preparation was made to present ourselves in the warmest and most hospitable, respectful manner. I will never forget the horror on my wife's face when our dog dragged its hind parts across the carpet in front of our guest in an apparent attempt to itch himself where he couldn't reach. How is it possible that our dog missed the requisite delicacy hospitality demanded? Answer: he's an animal! Animals are wonderful, but when men act like animals, everyone around them is in big trouble. We are not to put our own needs ahead of our wife or children. We are to honor our parents and do our best to remain **"aloof from strife."**[6] We are to spend ourselves and deny ourselves and exhaust ourselves in servant leadership of our loved ones. Don't worry if it's been awhile since you golfed or hunted or hung out with your buddies. Those things have a place and can fit in if/when possible, but refusing to make your own needs top priority is what makes you a man and not an animal. Much more on that later.

ACT LIKE A MAN MEANS DON'T ACT LIKE A BOY

I have five grandsons all under the age of five. Each one is a special joy but I must say they have reminded me of what I forgot since my kids were small. In a moment they can go from crying to laughing to fighting. They are loud, needy, and demanding. They are constantly on the search for new thrills, and their life revolves around the "itch" of the moment. Paul reports in 1 Corinthians 13:11 that **"when I was a child, I spoke like a child, I thought like a child, I reasoned like a child."** Kids are not able to figure that the sun and moon don't revolve around them. Men are supposed to know this. Acting like a man means developing a non-anxious presence that sees the big picture, remains calm in a crisis, and won't cave in under pressure. Godly men respond; they don't react. I confess to having taken far too long to learn that truth. God had to put me in some very hot water before I was forced to realize the importance of being silent when slandered, merciful when in the right, and lovingly patient when wronged. Any kid can join a meaningless scrap in the school yard, but Paul completes the passage I just quoted by saying, **"When I became a man, I gave up childish ways."**

ACT LIKE A MAN MEANS DON'T ACT LIKE A SUPERHERO

For some, forsaking the superhero persona may be the most important distinction. The above exhortations call a man to strength and stability, but those do not mean men don't feel things deeply and at times struggle profoundly. We are not Ironman. Every man needs a place to be open and vulnerable with brothers leaning together upon the Lord. I hope you have a small group of men you meet with regularly where you open your life up and seek the strength of numbers focused on a common goal. A circle of men who will hear your confessions and assure you of God's grace is a nonnegotiable for biblical manhood. None of us is everything God calls us to be and like James says, **"We all stumble in many ways."**[7] Acting like a man does not mean "acting." The term actually means "conduct yourself." It's the idea of intentionally choosing your behavior to reflect the best of what God calls us as men to be. We will talk about that on day two, but for now take a moment to answer the questions below and pray for God's help.

QUESTIONS FOR REFLECTION

1. What can you do today and this week to be a better servant-leader to your family?

2. In what ways might recent actions have appeared selfish, and what can you do today to correct that?

3. Do you agree that a man keeping his word and refusing to make excuses is a good summary of manhood? Why?

Prayer:

Dear Father in heaven,
Thank You for creating man in Your own image. Today I want
to be more conformed to Your image by more fully expressing
Your design for manhood. Please forgive me for the times I have
acted selfishly or passively and failed to cover and care for my
family as You have commanded. Please help me today to feel
the weight of my strength and to use it wisely and carefully
so those You have given to my care will sense my strong love
for them. Stir faith and hope in me now. I pray that the careful
reading of these forty studies will take me into a deeper
experience of Your plan for my life than I have ever known
before. In Jesus' name I pray, amen.

NEXT TIME:
MEET THE QUALITY MAN

2

A QUALITY MAN

*Give instruction to a wise man, and he will
be still wiser; teach a righteous man,
and he will increase in learning.*[1]

THE 1972 BLOCKBUSTER AND OSCAR WINNER *The Godfather*
is ranked by AFI as the #2 movie of all time and I admit to watching it
at least once a year. I love the scene where Sonny argues with Tom that
he needs a "wartime consigliere." I cry when the godfather gets shot and
cheer when his youngest son, Michael, a war hero, saves his dad from as-
sassins at the hospital. But best of all is the opening scene set on the day
the godfather's only daughter is to be married. Everyone is in the backyard celebrating, but Vito, the godfather, is stuck in his office, fulfilling
an apparent Sicilian pledge not to refuse any man on the day he gives his
daughter's hand in marriage.

Various characters come and go requesting help or vengeance from
the godfather. Then a family friend named Johnny comes in, some kind
of washed-up singer/actor, begging the godfather to secure him a particular movie role he has been refused. He cries into his hands, "I don't
know what to do. I don't know what to do." In that moment the ever-calm
Vito Corleone springs to his feet, pulls Johnny up by his hands, slaps him
across the face, and shouts, "YOU CAN ACT LIKE A MAN!" Later in

that scene he asks the singer, "Do you spend time with your family?" adding, "Good. Because a man who doesn't spend time with his family can never be a real man."

The scene resonates so deeply because we see a strong man who loves his family and sacrifices for them, exhorting a shallow man to follow his example and stop being so weak. In reality Vito's family is a mess and ends in ruin because of his sin, but his struggle to be a quality man for his family always grips and motivates me.

I have never met the dude who didn't at some level want to be a quality man. But for some reason in the pressure of the moment, we often cave in to behavior we despise. Why are so many men living the life of Vito Corleone; wanting more than anything to build a loving, loyal, God-fearing family, but watching in horror as we make choices that establish us as obstacles to the very things we would swear matter most to us? Not just in the movies but too often in real life, men tear down with their own hands the good that they set out to build. The phrase "his own worst enemy," is widely recognized because it occurs with a frequency that staggers the mind. What is wrong with us? Why do we resonate with the biblical words, **"For I do not do what I want, but I do the very thing I hate"**?[2] The answer is found at a much deeper level of manhood than the behavioral. The problem is in our very nature and only Christ can free us. As men we are broken and don't work right; we have fallen and can't get up. Like the mag wheel on a low profile sports car that has driven over a curb at high speed, men are *bent* and the fix is possible but not easy.

HOW WE GOT BENT

Adam, the first man, was declared by God to be **"good"** (Genesis 1:31) just after the Creator had breathed life into him. Fear of losing equality with God (falsely offered by the Enemy) and anger that a God who spoke of love would deprive him of any perceived benefit propelled Adam and the whole human race into what theologians call depravity. Depravity is the essence of our fallen nature and where we remain apart from an intervention by Christ. Depravity is an inability to choose the right and our constant inclination toward selfish sin. Like a cowlick that sticks up no matter how many times you slick it back, our nature as men is boldly bent toward badness. At the root of that bent are two powerful, sinful tendencies that must be conquered in Christ if we are to become quality men.

FEARFUL MEN ARE NOT QUALITY MEN

Get past the surface to the center of a man's soul and you will see that much of what is driving his depravity is fear. Like a strong wind can turn a spark into a forest fire, fear enflames much of what men do that is destructive.

- Bill is afraid of failing at work, so he lies about his product to hit sales quotas.
- Kyle fears rejection, so he isolates himself with negativity and avoidance.
- Tom fears being cheated, so he attacks everyone with suspicion and cynicism.
- Jeff fears being alone, so he is constantly cultivating elicit relationships.
- Randy fears being like his father but hears it in his voice as he yells at his kids.

We could easily feel compassion for men like these and may recognize ourselves in the generalized descriptions. But we must face the fact that a quality man overcomes his fear. Such a man refuses to be mastered by his anxiety and embraces the assurance that "**God gave us a spirit not of fear but of power and love and self-control.**"[3] A quality man examines his heart, exposing the fears that generate the lies that lead to sin.

What are you afraid of? Look directly at the action you most regret in the last year and answer this question: What were you afraid of? Confess fear as sin and confess the sin that fear produces. Ask God to replace that dread with a confident trust in His goodness. That's how a quality man acts. He faces and masters his fears instead of being mastered by them.

ANGRY MEN ARE NOT QUALITY MEN

I have struggled with anger in certain seasons of my entire adult life. I was emotional and impulsive as a student but very seldom angry. As I have gone from years to decades in ministry, I marvel at the battle with anger that has lessened with time but still calls for daily dependence on the Holy Spirit for self-control. I'm not a big fan of psychoanalysis, but I did seek out Dr. Garrett Higbee, our church counselor, and spent a few days with Dr. Henry Cloud for insight into how I can experience longer seasons of victory over outbursts of anger. Do you know what I am talking about? Have you heard yourself blow up at something seeming, upon reflection, to be small, but felt it wash over and consume you in a moment?

Anger, at least in my life, is driven by hurt. Early on in the life of the church, my deficiencies as a leader were magnified and force-fed to me by a few cofounders. As a young man still in my twenties, I was devastated. A few years later, that pattern repeated itself with other leaders, and by the third cycle, about fifteen years into the church's life, I had come to expect it. More and more, as I entered situations that seemed similar, I used anger to protect myself against hurt and betrayal. Instead of fearing a bad outcome in the face of needed confrontation, I ensured it through my anger and at least braced myself for the fallout. That is incredibly unhealthy and certainly not the characteristic of a quality man. To be successful in relationships, we must fully embrace the biblical observation that in all instances **"the anger of man does not produce the righteousness of God."**[4]

DEFEATING THE TWIN DANGERS

Acting like a man means getting victory over fear and anger. Fear is a self-protection we use to insulate ourselves from hurt by pulling back. Anger is self-protection we use to insulate ourselves from hurt by striking out. In both instances the answer is to face and forgive (more on forgiveness ahead) the hurt that expresses itself in fear or anger or both. How much good is left undone by failing to act like a quality man and conquer your fears? How much damage is suffered by those you love when you fail to act like a quality man and conquer your anger?

QUESTIONS FOR REFLECTION

1. Which is the tougher issue for me, fear or anger? Why?

2. When was the last time I used fear or anger to deflect a deeper hurt?

3. Who is most negatively impacted by my unresolved hurt and what should I do about it?

4. Who do I need to forgive and for what? Why have I not acted on this sooner?

Prayer:

Oh Father in heaven,
I long to live a life of quality manhood. Forgive me for the times
I have been conquered by hurt and acted out in fear and anger.
Grant me the courage to confess these same faults to family
and friends and coworkers who have suffered because of my
angry conduct or fearful failure to act. Give me eyes to see
the way I am affecting others and lead me into a more Christ-
honoring expression of manhood for Your glory and my own
good. I pray in Jesus' name, amen.

NEXT TIME:
WHEN A MAN LACKS QUALITY

3

NOT A QUALITY MAN

*A good name is to be chosen
rather than great riches.*[1]

PAUL CHRISTIE (NOT HIS REAL NAME) lives in the Midwest and runs his own business. He is handsome, known to many, and extremely charismatic. He lives in a large home with a lot of acreage, and by all appearances is highly successful. I have eaten at his table, slept in his home, and can tell you he is a worthless man.

I visit his city frequently and always seem to run into a recent patsy fleeced by Paul Christie. I have never met a person who knows Paul and doesn't think poorly of him. Everyone despises him and sadly, many hate him. His name pops up in conversation like a loud and foul bodily function at a baby dedication. When he's mentioned, people scratch their heads and squint with the look of someone about to dislodge a hornets' nest from the back porch. They know it needs to be done but search for a way to make it as painless as possible.

Paul is a churchgoer, shifting from church to church, each time wearing out his welcome more quickly than the last. He professes to follow Christ, but in this as in all things, he is a liar. He once ordered a trailer load of exotic furniture, but because the truck driver forgot to have him sign for the delivery, Paul claimed not to have received it and refused to pay. He has no mailbox, so when collectors arrived in person for the furniture payment, they were stopped at the private entrance as he relaxed in his stolen leather La-Z-Boy, gazing at the gate that locked them out.

Funny? Kind of pathetic, actually. But there he sits, two hundred pounds overweight, crushing his criminally gained furniture, weeping because his son is in prison, begging for my sympathy about his failing health, and demanding justice from everyone who has wronged him. Zero impulse control, he is narcissistic to the max, believing his own lies and bellowing constantly about blah, blah, blah. In no regard does Paul Christie act like a man nor can I find a person who has ever seen or experienced a better side of him. Paul is the opposite of quality; he is a worthless man.

Does that sound like a harsh assessment to you? Do I seem cruel to have reached such a firm conclusion? Yes, I know, God's grace is for everyone, but some people come to the place where they have refused it. The Spirit of God will not **"strive with man forever."**[2] Some people reach such a degree of resistance and refusal that God ceases trying to win their hearts. It's as sad as sad gets, and we should never presume to know who has gotten to a point of no return, but some surely have. In the Old Testament, Eli's sons, for example, definitely got to the place where it was too late for them. First Samuel 2:12 says, **"Now the sons of Eli were worthless men."** There you have it. And how did they reach this most scary of statuses? By following their father, who was the opposite of a quality man.

It seems that where the stakes are highest for quality men, both the best and the worst show up. This is certainly true in the area of church elders, where I've known through the years the highest and lowest examples of men placed as leaders of congregations of Christians.

Eli was a "local church preacher" at Shiloh, but he was the epitome of self-indulgence. He changed the holy rules given by God known as the Law, and he feasted on the choicest of meats from the people's religious sacrifices. If anyone resisted his servants, sent to secure his next meal (he was too fat to walk), Eli instructed them to take the food by force.[3] Eli, whose job it was to teach the people the wonder of God, was doing the opposite and treating the **"offering of the LORD with contempt."**[4] His brightest moment was his halfhearted warning to his sons who were having sex with women who came to serve the Lord and ended up servicing Eli's boys. **"No, my sons; it is no good report that I hear."**[5]

Apparently Eli's lame attempt to resist the evil of his sons' sexual addiction came nowhere close to what God means when He commands us to act like men. **"I am about to punish** [Eli's] **house forever, for the iniquity that he knew, because his sons were blaspheming God, and he did not restrain them."**[6]

STOP HONORING YOURSELF

A favorite movie scene of mine comes from *Gladiator*. Russell Crowe plays the part of the faithful General Maximus, who gains immense popularity through military conquests but refuses to recognize the emperor Commodus (Joaquin Phoenix). As the son of an emperor, Commodus gains the throne by murdering his ailing father, Marcus Aurelius. Commodus is so hugely insecure as ruler that he orders Maximus and his wife and son murdered. Maximus escapes and returns home to find his family slaughtered and passes out, only to be taken to Africa as a slave whose owner makes him into a minor league gladiator. Over many years, the warrior journeys back to Rome, fighting his way into the Coliseum until he again faces evil Commodus, who proves to be as treacherous and jealous as his father, Marcus Aurelius, was good.

As the story unfolds, Commodus tries to put Maximus to death but cannot because of his wide and growing popularity as an anonymous but brave fighter in the arena. To advance his incestuous intentions toward his own sister who loves Maximus, Commodus sets Maximus up for defeat in an impossible fight to the death with wild animals and soldiers. Incredibly (only in the movies), Maximus wins the battle and Commodus enters the ring, muttering through gritted teeth, "What am I going to do with you? You simply won't die." Maximus replies that he has only one person left to kill (obviously Commodus), but surrounded by soldiers pointing spears at him, he knows the time is not right and turns to walk away as the crowd cheers. In an effort to induce Maximus to fight while exhausted and massively outnumbered, Commodus says, "Your son squealed like a girl when they nailed him to the cross. And your wife moaned like a whore when they ravaged her again and again and again." In a mind-boggling show of strength and self-control, the men's faces are inches away as Maximus utters the ominous verdict, "The time for honoring yourself will soon be at an end." He bows and adds, "Highness."

Most action movie fans list this as one of the top movie lines of all time. It resonates with people because deep down we all know that the purpose of an elevated position is the good of others, not our own. Commodus was hated by the masses because he *honored himself* instead of denying his impulses and wants in order to benefit those his position existed to serve. Such was the self-serving attitude of Eli's sons.

WHO IS BEING HONORED?

The time came when it was too late for anyone to get through to Eli's sons. Explaining their ultimate inability to heed warnings they had rejected for so long, the Bible explains, **"It was the will of the Lord to put them to death."**[7] Eli had been too self-indulgent for too long. Through an unnamed prophet, God tells Eli the reason judgment is coming upon his family is his ongoing and unrelenting decision to **"honor your sons above me . . . those who honor me I will honor, and those who despise me shall be lightly esteemed."**[8]

Worthless men! They do exist both then and now and their defining characteristic starts with an inability to say no to themselves, but in the end becomes a stubborn refusal to say yes to God.

WHO'S YOUR DADDY?

Quality men are men under authority. Quality men listen and yield to the collective counsel of the wise and godly men around them. Whether your father was good or bad, loving or lecherous does not, in the end, give you license to do as you please. Our Daddy is God the Father and He expects that we will live in submission to His Word and His will for our lives.

Quality men can hear the voice of their own flesh demanding satisfaction, calling out for privilege and private pleasure. They hear the voice of temptation just as worthless men do, but they say NO! In God's strength and for His glory, a quality man denies himself for a higher purpose and says yes to the Lord. Every time you make a hard choice, take a higher road, or do the right thing, especially when your flesh and fans are calling out for you to do the opposite, right then, as you choose what honors God and not yourself, you are acting like a man, a quality man.

QUESTIONS FOR REFLECTION

1. Who is the most honorable man you know? Why do you hold that opinion of him?

2. Describe a time in your life you deeply regret when you honored yourself or someone you were called to lead above honoring God.

3. How does honoring our family above the Lord actually put them at risk?

4. Describe a time in your life you honored God above yourself. How did you feel about that decision subsequently? How do you view that decision now?

5. What quality masculine choice can you make today to better reflect what it means to "act like a man"?

Prayer:

Dear Father,
Thank You for Your grace at work in my life today. Thank You for patiently drawing me to the place where I want Your will more and more above my own. Thank You that I did not reach

the point where You ceased working in my life. I praise You for the opportunity to study this book as it presents Your Word and Your view of what it means to be a man. Forgive me for the many times I have honored myself above what I knew You wanted and what would be best for me and those I love. Please make me a quality man who serves the interests of others and does his best today to honor You in word and action. Thank You. In Jesus' name, amen!

NEXT TIME:

A LOOK AT A REAL QUALITY MAN

4

AND THE GOLD GOES TO . . .

*Do you not know that in a race all the
runners run, but only one receives the prize?
So run that you may obtain it.*[1]

ONE OF MY DRIVEWAY DREAMS as a kid was to play on the Canadian Olympic basketball team. There was no NBA in Canada when I was growing up, and it seemed the appropriate pinnacle of my athletic aspirations. For hours a day and years on end, I shot around the horn, trying to make every driveway basket twice, and imagining a big game on the line for Olympic glory. From where I grew up in London, Ontario, this was an over-the-top, pie-in-the-sky, fairy-tale fantasy, but I had it for many years. Only reluctantly did I let my basketball Olympic dream go as the realities of college tuition and my desire to buy a certain girl a diamond crowded out loftier daydreams.

Okay, let's be honest, it wasn't just the dame and the degree; I wasn't good enough. I was a top scorer on my high school team and a star on my Bible college b-ball team (sort of like being varsity in home school), but I wasn't even chosen as an all-star in my high school, let alone all-city or all-"state" (we had provinces), so I was a long, LONG way from making my country's Olympic team. I am 6 foot 3 and never made 6 foot 4, even in my Converse All Stars. I couldn't dunk, wasn't fast, and didn't play hard enough on defense. I was never considered for any basketball award, totaled my accolades at zero, and came about as close to representing my country in Olympic basketball as Bernie Madoff is to getting paroled. Except eventually he will get a parole hearing, and I was never within a country mile of wherever Olympic basketball decisions were made.

In my twenties and thirties I played in a lot of 3-on-3 tournaments and men's leagues. We won some games, but I was not the best player on any team I ever played on. Why is it so hard to tell the truth? I wasn't nearly good enough; I lacked athleticism and dedication and anything else you can lack going for Olympic gold. Not close, not even in the same solar system close, to being a good enough basketball player to realize my dream.

I am now in my fifties, and that is the most honest I have ever been about my basketball dream. Had you asked me back then, I had a lot of excuses for dropping my heart's desire:

- I had a bad coach who didn't pour into his players like other schools had.
- I hurt my ankle badly in my junior year and didn't get noticed.
- I was not part of the system of friends choosing friends, etc.
- I grew too late; I couldn't play in summer leagues for family reasons.
- I didn't want it bad enough, I had other priorities, and I had a lot of excuses.

BE HONEST IF YOU CAN

Do you relate to those excuses at all? Has there been a goal you set for yourself, an aspiration or personal improvement you aimed for but missed? Can you bring to mind a discipline you always thought you'd develop or a behavior you sincerely desire to adopt but haven't? Are there ways you thought you would have changed by now, but haven't? Sins you thought you'd shake, or learn to ignore, or find the strength to silence, but they still have your number, and when they phone you seem to always come running? Are you able to really be honest with yourself? If your answer is yes, you fail. No one is completely honest with himself, not in the moment at least. The closest we can come to total honesty is to admit our inability to be truthful with the face we see in the mirror. Personal honesty is too painful. It's like trying to pluck a pesky nose hair but always pulling away at the last second because the pain of the solution seems worse than the pain of the problem.

DESPERATELY WICKED

The Bible is less gracious about this condition, describing our capacity for personal candor in some pretty stark language. **"The heart is deceitful above all things, and desperately sick; who can understand it?"**[2] Do you realize what this means? It means we are so bent toward lying to ourselves that we can't solve our deepest problem or even recognize its magnitude. If you think you see how deceived you are about your true condition, then most assuredly you do not. Even if your behavior is more tucked in than the next guy, you are just as capable of sin at a behavioral level and just as culpable in your heart.

THE TYPICAL NEIGHBORHOOD

Drive through the typical neighborhood and stop on a block you like at random. Select any five houses in front of you and I will tell you about the men who live there. Statistically, there may not be a single quality man among them. In one or two of the homes, the original husband/father doesn't even live there anymore. He ran off with someone or in search of something, leaving those in the lurch he promised to love and lead 'til death. In the homes that remain, the three guys you could talk to if you knocked long enough have a list as long as their arm as to why they are where they are and the way they are. If there is anything "Olympic" about us, it's our ability to lie to ourselves.

- My parents left me, abused me, neglected me, malnourished me.
- Wrong schools, wrong teachers, wrong role models, wrong side of the tracks.
- Married a nagger, merged with a liar, met with a crisis, mired in mishaps.
- Reasons rationalized, validations voiced, varied vagaries, bottom line= EXCUSES

You could knock on a thousand doors in a million neighborhoods and not happen upon a single person who isn't making excuses for the reason they have failed at "Olympic Gold" in whatever capability or opportunity the Creator gave them.

THIS IS HOW YOU CHANGE

All change begins with a change of mind the Bible calls repentance. Repentance is detecting and destroying the rationalizations that led to me checking the sinful choice box in the first place. Repentance is what every biblical prophet was calling for because that is where a man begins to move from depravity to quality. Read the Old Testament and you'll notice the nonstop echo of calls for repentance. Ezekiel announced, **"Therefore I will judge you, O house of Israel, every one according to his ways, declares the Lord GOD. Repent and turn from all your transgressions, lest iniquity be your ruin."**[3] The diagnosis of sin had many symptoms, but the regimen for healing always began with repentance. The New Testament picks up the same theme. John the Baptist had a finely honed message for his audience—Repent! Jesus' first sermon had a familiar ring of repentance in it.[4] In the sermon that marked the birth of the church in Acts 2:38, Peter began his invitation to an audience eager to respond with the word *repent*. Later, the apostle Paul repeatedly wrote to believers about the crucial role of repentance.[5] And the last messages Jesus gave to John for the seven congregations mentioned in Revelation 2–3 include a common theme required of almost every church: repent.

APOSTLE PAUL: GIFTED AT REPENTANCE

It stands to reason that the further you have fallen into destructive sin and selfishness, the harder it is to turn back. But it is not impossible. One of the worst men to ever live was the Pharisee known as Saul of Tarsus. He was more self-righteous than a Five-Point Calvinist at a church growth seminar. He was more self-righteous than a homeschool mom at a gay pride parade. He was more self-righteous than a member of the Michigan militia at a congressional hearing on gun control. (Sorry, I got carried away.) Of himself at this time in his life, Paul said, **"If anyone else thinks he has reason for confidence in the flesh, I have more."**[6]

Saul (his Jewish name) was at first so sure that Jesus was not the Messiah that he had a brief career barging in on first-century home Bible studies across the nation of Israel and dragging the participants off to imprisonment, torture, and death. He was tireless in his blind, self-deceived persecution of the first Christians. Yet it all changed in a moment and Saul turned his life in a totally different direction. His self-deception was incinerated in a flash of grace on the road to Damascus when he came to embrace the truth about Jesus, whom he had labored to obliterate. Jesus Christ revealed Himself to Saul, renamed him Paul, and remade him into one of the most dedicated and quality men who have ever lived.

In future studies we will examine Paul's example in detail, but for now let his life serve as an example of repentance. Not a onetime event for the forgiveness of sin and gift of eternal life but a lifetime pattern of humility before a holy God. If you think repentance is something you only embrace at salvation and then abandon in a return to "saved but self-righteous" living, you couldn't be more wrong. Colossians 2:6 says, **"As you received Christ Jesus the Lord, so walk in him."** The path to salvation by faith travels down the way of repentance and we never leave that road.

How sad to see a worthless man who claims to know God confirm by running back to the road of self-righteousness that he never met Him. If Paul's self-deception and excuses could be obliterated, maybe the lies we tell ourselves can also be eclipsed in the presence of Christ who calls us to a continuous and even constant state of repentance. We do this, not to be forgiven but because at the cross our past, present, and future is forgiven once for all by the finished work of Christ. The purpose of continuous repentance in the life of a quality man is not a return to the crisis of salvation but part of what the Bible calls sanctification. Repentance is the choice to embrace the Holy Spirit's daily work of convicting us about ongoing sin. **"If we say we have no sin, we deceive ourselves, and the truth is not in us."**[7] If Paul can refer to himself as the **"foremost"** of sinners,[8] we can cultivate a constant and specific awareness of our need for grace. Quality manhood flows from genuine humility and continuous confession of personal need for the cleansing and healing mercy of Jesus Christ in matters a whole lot tougher than admitting you never really had a chance at Olympic Gold.

QUESTIONS FOR REFLECTION

1. What area of pride have you most shielded from total honesty?

2. Why do you think we find it so hard to be honest with ourselves?

3. When have you been most honest about your own sin? What brought you to that point?

4. What is the biggest lie you have told yourself about yourself and for how long?

5. Who is the most honest and humble man you have known? How might you begin to emulate him?

Prayer:

Father in heaven,
Thank You for the grace You have shown to me in Your Son
Jesus Christ, not only in saving me but also in guiding me

toward sanctification. I come to You today asking You to free me from the self-deception we all battle. Show me my sin and shortcomings as You see them. I welcome a deeper work of Your Spirit in my heart and pray for a greater humility in hearing and heeding the feedback I get from others. Guard my heart because I so easily run to excuses and defensiveness. Grant to me a new season of growth and change as I proceed through these studies and connect with other men on the same journey. Thank You for never giving up on me. In Jesus' name, amen.

NEXT TIME:
THE DESTROYER OF ALL THINGS QUALITY

5

"WHAT ARE YOU LOOKING AT?"

Be not wise in your own eyes.[1]

HE'S THE FURTHEST THING FROM A CUTE LITTLE red dragon with pointy tail, horns, and a pitchfork. He is the devil, Beelzebub, the serpent of old, the accuser of the brethren, Satan, the deceiver, and father of lies, and he comes to us as an angel of light.[2]

Light in the Bible speaks of truth. Jesus said, **"I am the light of the world."**[3] John wrote, **"Men loved darkness rather than light, because their deeds were evil."**[4] When Scripture describes Satan as an angel of light, it should make the hair on your neck stand up with terror. Man's greatest enemy is most present when we are most certain he is not. He comes as an angel of light. Satan is working his deception through disguise. We think we are doing the right thing, taking the needed stand, fighting the most important foe, but if we are not careful, extremely wise, and cautious, we are doing the opposite. Intending to advance the agenda of our King, we slip very easily into fighting the Lord and assisting satanic schemes. In every section of this book, we will spend one study assessing how Satan deceives us into believing we do well even when we fail to act like men.

DECEIVING THE QUALITY MAN

My wife, Kathy, comes from the so-called wrong side of the tracks, and it has been one of the best things in my ministry. She is not fooled by phonies, and while very sweet and loving to all, she is street-smart in a way that has saved me more than once. Her father, Dennis, was in prison when she was born and divorced from her mom before she can remember. Her dad passed away in a construction accident at the age of forty-seven. He was a roofer and sadly fell to his death while drinking on the job. Though her father invested a lot of himself during Kathy's adolescence, she mainly grew up in the home of her stepfather, Ralph. Ralph is a former military French Canadian, a legend in many ways. He is a man of immense friendship, constant generosity, marital infidelity, frequent altercations with the law, and constant alcohol abuse. Dennis and Ralph were the best of friends as the first and second husbands of Kathy's mom and actually got drunk together at our outdoor wedding, hiding mickeys of vodka in the tank of my parents' toilet for retrieval during the reception. Ralph is not a tall man, but I have pulled him out of a few fights, and I know he saved my life at least once. Ralph would give you the shirt off his back and if you crossed him would kill you.

My first summer of marriage, Ralph, a newly elected representative of the United Auto Workers union, got me a job at the Ford Assembly plant where he spent his entire career. Still in Bible college, I was happy to have a job with good income to pay the bills. What I didn't see coming was that although he worked for the union and could get me a job, the animosity between labor and management showed up in the job they gave the son-in-law of the union rep. With a Grinch-that-stole-Christmas grin, the shift manager assigned me to the body shop prepping doors on the ten-hour night shift. Every time I fell behind the line in my job of riveting options to the passenger doors of Crown Victorias, I was chorused by the other workers with a torrent of sewage mouth, which hardened me in a hurry to the discomfort of profanity. The centerfolds and worse that they hung around their work areas, the alcoholism and drug abuse on every break, the constant barrage of persecution born in their disdain for how I got the job and multiplied when they discovered I was in training to be a preacher, all combined to make those months on the job nearly unbearable, but in the end extremely educational.

When I stand up to preach each weekend, I remind myself that I look into the faces of men who work each day in environments like the one I experienced that summer in college. The gospel of Christ is for people who come from where my wife did. Growing up with Christian parents and grandparents, my minuscule adolescent detours into the world didn't bring me remotely close to what Kathy grew up seeing and what I sampled that summer working the night shift.

VERY FEW MEN ARE QUALITY MEN

Our church surely has its share of liars and hypocrites. I don't want you to think I am naïve. The reality, however, is that liars and hypocrites stand out at church because most Christian men are not that way. They are all seeking at some level to become the quality men Christ calls us to be. I don't know a single man in our church who wouldn't willingly verbalize a strong desire to act like a man.

However, that is not the case in our world. Men are selfish stinkers, kid beaters, and wife cheaters. Many are addicted to porn. Many steal at work, claiming they are "just taking what's coming to them" and more, whether they earned it or not. They are lying, conniving, and coveting idolaters, out for themselves and gladly devouring anyone who gets in their way. YES, there are exceptions, but to readily find a truly quality man in the marketplace who is loving his family and living for a purpose beyond himself, giving a day's work for a day's pay every day and finding ways to be generous and thoughtful to others, not so much. Men who are faithful to their wives and kids in thought, word, and action? Very hard to find. And here is the lie exposed . . .

GOD DOESN'T GRADE ON THE CURVE

Remember how, say the high school science teacher, would give an exam that was so incredibly hard that everyone wanted to choke him as they left the class and stood in the hallway afterward shaking their heads in disgust? Remember too, how the best teachers would realize their mistake and raise all the grades evenly? We called that grading on the curve, where they considered the performance of others in determining what your grade should be.

Hebrews 9:27 reports, **"It is appointed for man to die once, and after that comes judgment."** Every man, good or evil, is headed to an appointment with the Creator of the universe who will judge us all by the very same standard. The fact is that God demands perfection and all of us fall incredibly short. The good news of the gospel is that through faith in Jesus we can be forgiven our sin and assured of a place in heaven based upon God's promise. That glorious truth, however, does not mean that we will not answer to God. Some say there will be one judgment with two parts, others insist the judgment of believers and nonbelievers will be separate. I am not sure, but of this I am confident, **"each of us will give an account of himself to God."**[5] Because we live and work with a lot of men who are far from quality men, we can easily begin to think that God is like our high school science teacher, pulling up the lower marks by grading on the curve. Please hear this. God does not grade on the curve. The fact that you are a better man than some of the worthless guys you rub shoulders with will mean nothing on the day you stand before your Creator to be judged by His holy standard.

SATAN'S LIE TO MEN

By putting you constantly in touch with men who don't love their wives as you strive to do, Satan whispers that you are doing well because you are not like those other men. Because you are working with men who use language you don't and profane a God you seek to worship; because you see in the news and read about men who do things you would never dream of doing on your worst day, sinful actions you would rather die than commit; you can begin to think you are a quality man when in reality you are not—not by God's standard, not to the degree that you could be, that He longs for you to be. I am writing this book to help you but find myself deeply convicted by what I have just written. Let me say it first: I am not the quality man that I want to be, that I know God wants me to be, not yet.

We must silence the lies of our enemy and discipline our minds to remember that God is not comparing us to other men. God has declared, **"You shall be holy, for I am holy."**[6] As you hear news or witness sinful struggles, discipline your mind to avoid self-righteous judgment and practice saying with other humble believers, "There, but for the grace of God, go I." Be alert to any prideful feelings of superiority in comparing yourself to others, something Satan is provoking you to fall into. As long as the Enemy of your soul can have you feeling superior to the next guy, he has successfully insulated your heart from evaluating your own actions and priorities according to God's standard of what it means to act like a quality man.

QUESTIONS FOR REFLECTION

1. What behavior characterizes the worst men you know?

2. In what ways have you battled, at least on an attitude level, the very same things?

3. Why is it essential that we hold ourselves to a higher standard than what we see around us?

4. What good results from the practice of being harder on ourselves than others?

5. Why do Christians seem to struggle more than nonbelievers with judging others?

Prayer:

Dear Father,
Thank You for giving me the interest and energy to take stock

of my own life and where I am in regard to Your holy standard. I see my tendency to compare my actions and priorities to others and think more highly of myself than I should. I see how pride and avoidance of some "bigger sins" can demotivate my pursuit of being the quality man You have called me to be. I choose to renew my pursuit of truly acting like a man in Your eyes. Forgive my indifference to the immense need for transformation in my own heart. Thank You for the grace that allows me to begin afresh, and grant me the courage to place no limits on how You shape and change my life for Your glory. In Jesus' precious name, amen.

NEXT TIME:
GOD WEIGHS IN ON QUALITY

6

TRULY—AS GOOD AS IT GETS

The Rock, his work is perfect, for all his ways are justice. A God of faithfulness and without iniquity, just and upright is he.[1]

TRUE CONFESSION. OKAY, LET ME have a moment of total honesty and confess that I am not a fan of perfectionists. I don't weigh every word before I speak it. I forget stuff, regret stuff, and would bet all my stuff that perfectionists cause a lot of pastors' palpitations of the heart. I searched my skin for scars not caused by perfectionist fallout from my faults and found none. As a preacher, my imperfections are many and broadly on public display. Generally I have received a ton of grace pastoring the same church for over twenty-six years, but that single kind of narrow-minded, my-way-is-the-right-way-all-the-way, all the time person—yeah, not a picnic for sure.

Their problem is in thinking they are perfect, which they do, but aren't. This becomes apparent each time they issue forth decrees, disdain, and disgust when their imagined perfection is contradicted. Worst of all is trying to tell a person who thinks they are perfect that they are actually condescending, confounding, or convoluted in their confusion. Good luck! Once their chosen target has been subjected to the corridor of filters they demand of every word or action as they rule from their throne room, there is no redress, no review, and no reconciliation. For those who assaulted their imagined superiority with the audacity to question perfection, the results won't be pretty. They truly believe they have achieved the status reserved for God alone.

ONLY GOD IS PERFECT

I studied all the words I could find to summarize the character and essence of our Creator, Father God, and it seems the best term is *perfect*. Only God is perfect! None of us comes within a country, not a country mile, but a whole country, in proximity to perfection. In fact, theologians, when speaking of God's nature, describe His traits as *perfections*. For example, Charles Hodge wrote, "The perfections of God, therefore, are attributes, without which He would cease to be God."[2]

While our God has many characteristics that we can share called communicable attributes, such as love, truth, and long-suffering, He also has a host of attributes that we cannot share. These are His incommunicable attributes, such as sovereignty, omniscience, and omnipresence. While He is infinitely more than we could ever be, He remains in totality and perfection what He is working to establish in us. The traits of our heavenly Father that can be reproduced in us are readily apparent from His Word. He expresses in His perfection what He calls us as men to become, beginning with this matter of acting like men, or being a quality man.

A GOD OF QUALITY

I told you about my wife's stepfather in the last study. Before he worked for the United Auto Workers union, he was just a guy on the assembly line doing what autoworkers do. Over time he progressed to one of the more cushy jobs away from the assembly line in quality control. I remember smiling as he described his final job in the water test area. Cars would be run through a high-pressure water booth, like a car wash, except that a fluorescent of some kind was added to the water. His job involved opening a door and shining a black light around the interior when it came out of the booth, searching for fluorescence, which would indicate a leak.

To hear Ralph tell the story, he had it down to a science. He would sit and read for 19–21 minutes (a car a minute) then run to the head of the line, scanning each car in about ten seconds all the way to the door of the water booth. Leaks were extremely rare, or so he said, so mainly he just sat and read Louis L'Amour Westerns, jumping up for three minutes three times an hour to do his quality check. My guess is that a lot of people took their cars back to the dealership for door adjustments the first time they drove in the rain. Not exactly what the company had in mind during the days their slogan said, "At Ford, Quality Is Job 1."

IMPERFECTION IS NOT ADMIRABLE

To be sure, perfection can be pesky in another human being, but we cannot let our disdain for those who assess everything and everyone keep us from the importance of analyzing what we are doing and why. Our heavenly Father is perfection, has perfections, and assures perfection in all He does. During the first six days of the universe, as the Creator called forth space, time, planets, peninsulas, and porcupines, He stopped at the end of each day to review the quality of what He had done. Every phase of His creation He saw was **"good."**[3] And somehow, in spite of how we know the story unfolded, God included mankind in His conclusion that all He created was good.

Given God's obvious interest in the quality of what He does, and given the fact that His only mistakes involve—hmm . . . He never made one—can we afford to review our actions and priorities less than He does? Shouldn't our first promise to God and those we love be our determination to fulfill the role established by God for each and every man? To do that job to the best of our ability is the essence of what it means to be a quality man.

A QUALITY MAN I KNOW

You may recognize the name Jerry Jenkins from his smash-hit Left Behind novels. But long before he became famous, he wrote helpful books.

You wouldn't know he's a world-class author by looking at him. The quality of a man is not measured by notoriety or success.

The first time I met Jerry Jenkins, we were on a golf course, and he was so bad. In fact, he doesn't even golf anymore. But at the time, he was putting on a determined effort to become an excellent, confident golfer. He gave up on that. I think the choice was wise. Jerry is a man's man, but he is inept at golf, so apparently you don't need to be good at every sport to be a quality man.

The reason I think Jerry is a quality man is because of his character. I have watched him in a lot of situations—many of them not conducive to bringing out the best in anyone. He has been an example of grace and rock-solid manhood. I have seen what he is like in private, relating with his wife and his grown children. I have seen what he is like in a crisis, leading effectively. He is a man's man. I'm privileged to call him a friend. I hope you're on your way to being such a quality man.

QUESTIONS FOR REFLECTION

1. How does the truth that your heavenly Father is perfect impact you today?

2. Do you find God's perfection motivating to your growth or overwhelming? Why?

3. Imagine if a light were shone on your character—what leaks would be revealed?

4. List those areas most needing attention as you pursue quality manhood.

5. Name a specific action you can take today to advance your pursuit of quality manhood.

Prayer:

Dear God,
You are just and right in all You do, a God of perfection. I bow before You today as a man with many flaws. Please give me strength to pursue the fullest expression of Your design for me as a man. Give me wisdom to see the way my faults are burdens to others and give me courage to face and work on those imperfections. I am thankful for Your persistent pursuit of me despite my shortcomings and sin. Forgive me for being indifferent to my faults as I gratefully receive Your grace today. Thank You for renewing my passion to be a quality man. For the glory of Jesus' name, amen.

NEXT TIME:
JESUS AS THE ULTIMATE QUALITY MAN

7

DISNEYLAND QUALITY

For in him all the fullness of God was pleased to dwell, and through him to reconcile to himself all things, whether on earth or in heaven, making peace by the blood of his cross.[1]

I AM SITTING IN A CAFÉ IN THE Hollywood Studios theme park of Disney World in Orlando, Florida. My third park in three days as Kathy and our three married children happily spend our family vacation enjoying the area with five delightful grandsons (delightful, that is, except right before nap time).

I am absolutely floored, I mean blown away by the quality of all things Disney. Not that I haven't been here before. We came on our honeymoon, and we visited for special dinners once or twice a year during the nineties when I was on the board of a wonderful mission organization called Pioneers. When our kids were small, Kathy worked as a school crossing guard, saving for several years so we could bring our kids to Disney. We counted every penny but made it work by driving down and staying in a trailer at the camp Pioneers owned. Annual pastor retreats for Harvest Bible Fellowship are held at our Harvest church plant in Orlando, and we usually spend an afternoon walking around one of the Disney parks. All that to say, I have been to Orlando probably fifty times in the past thirty years, and many of those trips included a stop at Disney.

So why is my mouth hanging open this time? Why am I astounded at the immense and unceasing quality of the buildings, the cleanliness, the friendliness, the imagination and vision and incalculable focus on quality? It's partly because we became vacation club members awhile back and are staying on the grounds getting the whole experience. But more than that, as a young adult, I had no idea, I mean not a shred of a sense of the kind of effort that goes into making anything ring the quality bell, one time. Back then I had not even entered the universe of understanding such an ocean of unceasing and expanding quality like the twenty-five thousand acres of Disney World, twice the size of Manhattan. It is absolutely mind-boggling to consider the complexity of this place that has closed only three days in its history, yet maintains and increases excellence constantly. Further, it opened for the first time more than five years after its founder died. The passion for quality that he put into his family and staff carried and still carries the vision forty years later. Wow wow wow!

QUALITY—FOR NOW VS. FOREVER!

Walt Disney died at sixty-five from lung cancer. A chain smoker all his life, he lived only a few weeks after his diagnosis. Walt Disney created, past tense, some quality temporal things in his relatively short lifetime. Jesus Christ, who existed before time and created all we see around us, came to this world two thousand years ago, and the quality of His enduring incarnation is still impacting lives today. Comparing Disney to Jesus Christ is like comparing a grain of sand to the Sahara, like comparing a speck of moondust to the One who called forth the planets and the stars. I use the comparison only for this reason: Do you recognize quality when you see it? Not just quality work as in Disney's case but quality character?

Do you notice and applaud the capacity to do the right thing, in the right amount, at the right moment, and for the right reasons? That is the quality Jesus Christ personifies for us and we do well to act like men and emulate Him.

DOING THE RIGHT THING IS QUALITY CHOICE

Life is a series of choices. As men, we are faced with a barrage of choices every single day. Can I afford that? Must I address my son's behavior or should I let it pass? How will my time be divided up? How does God want me to serve? Who will I share Christ with and how? Is this an acceptable form of entertainment for a Christ-follower? Where will this road take me and will I be happy when I get there? Solomon observed **"the little foxes that spoil the vineyards."**[2] So it is with our lives as men. The little things not addressed, dealt with, handled, or held up become big things that can bring devastation.

An offense not resolved can fester and become bitterness as Proverbs 18:19 says: **"A brother offended is more unyielding than a strong city."** A priority not firmly established can fall to lesser things. **"A double-minded man [is] unstable in all his ways."**[3] A discipline not maintained can bring a weakness and yielding that could destroy multiple generations in my family. **"The LORD, the LORD, a God merciful and gracious, slow to anger, and abounding in steadfast love and faithfulness, keeping steadfast love for thousands, forgiving iniquity and transgression and sin, but who will by no means clear the guilty, visiting the iniquity of the fathers on the children and the children's children, to the third and the fourth generation."**[4] Jesus personifies quality choices: **"What will it profit a man if he gains the whole world and forfeits his soul?"**[5]

DOING THE RIGHT THING IN THE
RIGHT AMOUNT IS QUALITY CONTROL

Lots of men do right things but they fall into an extreme, even single-minded focus. I knew a man years ago who exhausted himself serving students in our ministry. Then it came out that he had been secretly unfaithful to his wife for years and ended up losing his kids and marriage. This man helped a ton of young people follow a Savior he wasn't following himself. He was such a sad example of a guy doing right things, but in the wrong amount, while covering up the wrong things.

Acting like a man, a quality man, has to involve conscious quality control. I see families focus on their kids to the point of idolatry, failing to apply the lesson from Abraham and Isaac that putting our kids in the place of God puts them at risk.

I have watched many men exhaust themselves in their careers making a boatload of money and then trying to give that money away to ministry and family in a desperate attempt to get back what they gave up in getting that money in the first place. There is no quality without balance.

Jesus exemplifies the importance of quality control of our quality choices by the way He often stepped aside from healing and teaching to attend to His inner life. **"And rising very early in the morning, while it was still dark, he departed and went out to a desolate place, and there he prayed."**[6]

DOING THE RIGHT THING IN THE
RIGHT AMOUNT AT THE RIGHT TIME IS QUALITY TIMING

Problems arise with our God-given gifts and abilities when we want to do them all the time. Let me throw myself under the bus to make it clear what I mean. I am gifted by God as a truth-teller. My best contribution to Christ and His kingdom is telling people the truth of God's Word in a way they can understand and apply. In weekly doses from the pulpit, that mostly goes great. The problem comes when I try to use my gift with an individual. The Bible exhorts **"the anger of man does not produce the righteousness of God,"**[7] but I have certainly tried. When I see people I love making a mess in choices that are the furthest thing from quality, I have found it terrifically difficult to sit by and watch. Surely a confrontation, a constant pleading, or a careful insistence will arrest their attention and avert disaster. Nope, not that often. More likely you get pulled into the canoe as they try to take you over the falls with them. Or worse, they turn the focus back on you in complete denial. Only the pain of seeing clearly how I failed others by trying in every situation to do what I do best has taught me the wisdom of withholding my gifts as I wait on God's timing.

Maybe your gift is mercy, or teaching, or leadership, or service. Sometimes the "quality man" choice is to do nothing for now. Jesus personified quality timing when He ceased ministry in a certain city: **"And he did not do many mighty works there, because of their unbelief."**[8]

RIGHT THING, RIGHT AMOUNT, RIGHT TIME
AND REASONS IS TOTAL QUALITY MANHOOD

We must not think that action alone is successful Christ-following. In God's eyes, the motives behind our actions are of paramount importance. You can want a godly family or a successful career or a low handicap or a beautiful lawn, but if you want them for yourself and not the glory of God, it's a fail.

Jesus wants to change our hearts and that gets to issues far deeper than right behavior. Paul said, **"The sins of some people are conspicuous, going before them to judgment, but the sins of others appear later."**[9] What this means is that those who fail in action are frequently exposed here on earth, but those who do right things for wrong reasons are often not discovered until the next life.

Jesus personified quality manhood in His selfless sacrifice for our sins but He condemned hidden, evil motivations when He echoed His Father's sentiments: **"This people honors me with their lips, but their heart is far from me."**[10] Don't be "that guy" who doesn't pursue quality throughout his life.

QUESTIONS FOR REFLECTION

1. Where have you seen quality manhood displayed in your everyday life?

2. What specifically do you note in that man's example that you can emulate?

3. What is harder for you, right actions or right timing? Why?

4. In what ways is our challenge easier or harder than the life Jesus lived?

5. Describe a pastor or spiritual leader you have watched as a quality man.

Prayer:

Dear Father in heaven,
Thank You for giving Jesus Christ as an example of what it means to be a quality man. Thank You that in His life and death I can see what You are asking of me. Give me wisdom and strength as I persevere in the roles You have called me to carry out. Keep my heart close to Your Son in word and action and let my every choice be made with Your honor and glory as my heart's only desire. Give me faith to believe that I lose nothing in that choice and instead find everything that I have searched for so long. I love You, in Jesus' name, amen.

NEXT TIME:
HOW THE HOLY SPIRIT BRINGS QUALITY

8

LET YOUR PARTNER TAKE THE LEAD

*For all who are led by the Spirit
of God are sons of God.*[1]

I'VE ALWAYS BEEN A GOLFER. Since I was fourteen years old and my father bought a kid who batted and played hockey left-handed a garage sale half-set of right-handed clubs, I have loved the game of golf. I remember protesting, "But Dad, I swing left-handed." He replied, "Everything in golf is for right-handers, son; learn to swing right-handed." Such a sensitive man, ha ha. Anyway, I did learn to play right-handed and have played often. Until the last three or four years, golf was what I looked forward to doing when Midwest weather permitted.

In recent years though, maybe as a release from the frustrations of difficult people, I have taken to hunting. I am not like those guys who wait for hours to sneak up on a turkey with an arrow and a bow. For me, it's all about the killing, nothing subtle or too strategic, just get the game in the scope, breathe out slowly, and pull the trigger. I have taken down some prize bucks and an elk or two, more recently turning my attention to hunting a bear in the panhandle of Idaho. All that to say, there is something really awesome about sitting for hours in a tree stand, only to see a bear amble up to the bait, oblivious to your presence. The gun is raised, the head is lowered, and the eye blinks to see close-up through the scope. The crosshairs get shifted to just behind the shoulder blade and slowly, ignoring a pounding heart, you squeeze the trigger.

LET'S GET FOCUSED

I hope that after the first seven studies, quality manhood is in the crosshairs for you. But how do you keep pulling the trigger and "killing it" day after day, week after week? As I have been writing about quality men and how they act, you may have been feeling a bit overwhelmed. You know the struggle to make one good choice, let alone to keep making them day after day. You see the negative example of a worthless man like Eli and agree that you want a better legacy for yourself and your kids than he left behind. You are inspired by the example of Paul and frankly intimidated by the example of Christ and His infinite expression of quality manhood. If becoming a more quality, God-honoring expression of what it means to act like a man was easy, everyone would be doing it. In fact, we can begin to feel like the goal is unattainable and fall quickly into passive wanting versus active pursuit of this worthy objective.

GOOD NEWS

1. The call of God makes our goal crystal clear: to be quality men, accomplishing God's purpose for manhood.

2. We want to emulate the example of Jesus Christ in our leadership of all He has entrusted to us, relying on His grace to stay motivated when we fall short.

But where is the wisdom to make the toughest decisions? Where is the actual strength to choose unselfishly when flesh is demanding immediate gratification?

The answer is the Holy Spirit. I hope you haven't been turned off to the Holy Spirit by some wild-eyed fanatic, frantically falling down in a frenzy. I hope the term *Holy Spirit* doesn't bring to mind some tomato-faced preacher on TV shouting Hoooooly Ghoooossst and dragging out the syllables of an ancient translation in a way that simulates a horror movie more than help.

God's greatest gift to us since the cross of Christ has been the Holy Spirit. He is the third person of the Trinity, equally and entirely personal, every bit as much a part of the Godhead as the Father and Son. He is sent by the Father, according to Ephesians 1:14, as a deposit, the earnest money that demonstrates God's intention to make good on every salvation promise.

As a follower of Jesus through faith in Him, the Holy Spirit is your only hope of ever consistently acting like a man. He is the courage to make right choices, the guide toward truth and away from error, the source of our comfort, and the provider of our strength. His primary tool is the Word of God.

WATCHING GOD'S SPIRIT WORK

When Joe Screwdriver shows up at Harvest, it's often under some duress. Maybe he lost a bet with his wife or he decided to find out what was happening in her life. But he's not sure. And the first week, he sits cross-armed and leaning back—observing. He's here, but in the *I'm not participating* mode. But when weeks become months, I see the Holy Spirit using God's Word to transform Joe Screwdriver. First he unfolds his arms; he relaxes. And then he kind of leans forward. At first he projects, *"I'm not singing, dude. I am flat-out not singing. You can't make me. I'm going to show you I don't like what's happening right now."* But we watch him. We observe how God changes the heart of people.

And this is how He does it. Psalm 19:7 says, **"The law of the LORD is perfect, converting the soul"** (NKJV). God's Word is so powerful it is able to take an unsaved, unregenerated, uninterested, hard-hearted Joe Screwdriver and absolutely turn that guy's life around! Spin him on his head. Raise him up a new person. Arms once folded get lifted and lips once sealed now smile in praise to God.

In what ways can you say, "I'm a different person because of the impact God's Word has made in my life"?

Here is another result of the Spirit's application of God's Word to Joe's life: wisdom expands. Psalm 19:7 also says, **"The testimony of the LORD is sure, making wise the simple."** The word *testimony* pictures God as witnessing to Himself. If you want to know what God is like, it's nice to hear from people. But what about God Himself taking the witness stand and saying, "This is what I'm like. This is who I am. This is what I will do for you." The **"testimony of the LORD"** is God bearing witness to Himself. God is not required to tell us about Himself, but He does. If He chose to remain hidden, we wouldn't have a clue, but His love and His plans for us ensure that He lets us know what we need to know. Ultimately He has spoken through the written Word and His Son, Jesus Christ.[2]

Psalm 19:7 affirms the following about God's self-revelation: **"The testimony of the LORD is sure."** It's dependable and durable. The NIV says it's **"trustworthy."** The word is similar to the term transliterated "amen" in English. We could read this phrase, **"The testimony of the LORD is amen."** It is the real thing; authentic; consistent with God's character. His Word is reliable. But you're wondering, *"How reliable is the Bible exactly?"*

I'd like to answer that question—right from the source. The testimony of the Lord is so sure that it **"makes wise the simple"** (v. 7). This is a widely applicable necessity, you see, because Joe Screwdriver's setback is one we all share. We've all been like him. Our problem isn't *just* stubbornness and hard-heartedness. We are also naïve and foolish. The idea behind this word *simple* is actually an *open* or *unguarded mind*. In today's language we would say a simple person has no mental firewalls, virus software, or wise discrimination. The simple person is easily led astray. Their mind is like a house with the front door *and* back door open. An idea comes in and the simple person thinks, *"That's amazing! I guess that's what I'll believe."* But then another thought blows in and they switch mental gears: *"I'm going to follow this guy now. He's the latest author featured on all the talk shows."* A simple person can't hang on to what matters because they don't have the capacity to feel the weight of what is substantive or notice the influence of what is light, fluffy, and foolish. They have no discernment. The world may have high praise for the so-called open-minded person, but godly wisdom controls access to the mind. G. K. Chesterton said, "The problem with a lot of open minds is that they need to be closed down for repairs!"

Now *that* is a big problem. And we have all been that open, deer-in-the-headlights kind of simple person. But the testimonies of the Lord are so sure that they can make a foolish, vacillating, undiscerning person into a wise person. My friend Joe Screwdriver? He used to be an easy mark for the world—but he's so wise now. The things he says, the insights he has, and the understanding he brings to conversations are remarkable. "*Where did this come from?*" We know where it came from. God's Word is pouring wisdom into Joe's life just like it can pour into yours and mine. The Holy Spirit has been doing His good work to make Mr. Screwdriver a quality man.

QUESTIONS FOR REFLECTION

1. Describe two or three specific ways God has been working on your life through His Word.

2. What are some of your personal observations of the Holy Spirit at work in those around you?

3. If someone called you a quality man, what do you think they would be referring to the most? In what ways might they suggest you can improve?

Prayer:

Father,
Thank You not only for challenging me to act like a man but also for giving me Your Spirit as an indwelt reminder and source of strength to guide and help me to be the man You want me to be. Thank You for Your Word and for the way You use it to change me, shape me, and give me wisdom. Please help me increase my reliance on Your Word and my willingness to obey

what You show me in those pages. Improve my quality as a man as I hide Your Word in my heart that I might not sin against You. I ask You for these things in the name of Your Son, Jesus, who saved me by His cross and sealed me by the Holy Spirit, amen.

NEXT TIME:

WE ACT LIKE MEN WHEN WE LEARN TO BE URGENT

BE WATCHFUL

9

KEEP YOUR HEAD UP

But know this, that if the master of the house had known in what part of the night the thief was coming, he would have stayed awake and would not have let his house be broken into.[1]

IT IS ETCHED IN MY MIND WITH THE KIND of urgency only an angry coach can give a collegiate. My high school football coach had a single strategy to motivate our participation: angry intimidation followed by punishment for failure. I was a linebacker and he would scream 'til he was hoarse, "Keeeeeep youuurrrr heeeaad up!!!" If your head was down, the offensive lineman pulling left or right on a running play would catch you unaware and leave you spun around on your keister with a perfect view of the opposing team's touchdown. Effective coaching to be sure, because I can't speak the words "keep your head up" without hearing "Ted" and fearing the outcome of failing to do so. Keep your head up—great advice in coaching and in life. Why then are so many men stumbling through life, blindsided by what is happening all around them?

WATCH

Inspired by the Holy Spirit, one characteristic of a quality man—the first command to be added to the core exhortation, act like men—is *watch*! Like the other four in our theme verses 1 Corinthians 16:13–14, this is a present imperative calling for constancy and a continued state of mind rather than a onetime action that is finished and done with. In other words, acting like a man means always being on the alert, ever aware, at the ready constantly, paying close attention continuously.

Back when Kathy was in nursing school, she lived about forty-five minutes away in the small city of Woodstock. My fiancée at the time, she shared an apartment on the top floor of a four-story walk-up with her cousin Cindy. The newspapers that fall were headlining a murderer who raped and stabbed his victims, gaining access to their apartments by climbing up balconies and entering through the unlocked sliding door. Hardly anyone, it seemed, locked their patio doors on higher floors.

I will never forget the immediate knot in my stomach when Kathy called to report on their young landlord, who had been hovering in the entranceway, hoping to catch their attention, knocking frequently on their door, requesting access to investigate various purported "utility problems." He refused to be deterred even after their firm requests to be left alone. With terror in her voice, she shouted through her half breaths that he had scaled to their apartment from outside and was knocking on the window.

"Call the police!" I yelled as I ran for the car, picked up Kathy's father, and drove forty miles in about twenty minutes. Straight to his door we went, pounding 'til he came out. Trust me when I say we were persuasive. I'll let your imagination fill in the blanks according to your comfort level, but as a result, he never spoke to them again and looked away whenever he saw them coming or going from school that semester. By Christmas, Kathy moved back to the comfort and protection of home. If you know how you feel and what to do when you perceive that your family is threatened, you understand the watchful state of mind that God made a man to exhibit continuously.

If you haven't been watchful as God commands, you might think me overly dramatic to say an enemy is pounding on the door to your home. If you have been lulled into a state of slumber by selfish choices and silly hobbies, you might be insulted by the suggestion that most Christian men are asleep; nevertheless it is true. Most men are not alert, not paying attention, and not watching out for their families as God commands them to. I don't know a comfortable way to wake some of them up.

WATCHMEN

I wonder at times if industrialization hasn't deprived men of a lot that God created them to do. Men were not made to sit in offices and talk endlessly on the phone. Men were not designed for mindless, repetitive work that sacrifices every spark of creativity and initiative for an all-too-meager paycheck. Men were made for war; designed to struggle and strive to protect and provide. Most of the sports and leisure that appeal to men have grown up around what's pent up inside of us. The problem is that we are not supposed to be watching men fight it out in the Octagon or on the football field; we are supposed to be in the game ourselves.

In the Old Testament times, the cities in Israel were fortified with stone walls and battlements. Around the clock, men were posted as sentinels to scan the horizon for impending danger and to sound the alarm at the first sign of approaching threats. Praying is good and needed, but your job isn't done when you have asked God for protection over your family. You have to do your part.

"And we prayed to our God and set a guard [watchman] **as a protection against them day and night."**[2] We have to resist the urge to see these guys as special or unique. They were men just like you and me, the Joe Screwdrivers of their day, doing their job, watching for opposition against their community, acting like men. Not special or unique; typical dudes you would join to build a deck or play darts. **"Mattaniah, Bakbukiah, Obadiah, Meshullam, Talmon, and Akkub were gatekeepers standing guard at the storehouses of the gates."**[3] Nothing worse than preachers who lose their own kids, or cops who protect the city but leave their families vulnerable, or firemen who put out fires for others but are arsonists in their own homes. It's so very sad when we do the job for others and fail to do it for those who need us most. The Old Testament watchmen weren't like that. Nehemiah 7:3 says, **"And while they are still standing guard, let them . . . appoint guards . . .** *some in front of their own homes."*

Your highest loyalty after the Lord is to your family. Your first priority after God is your wife then your kids. You, metaphorically, are standing at the door of your home and watching to make sure nothing enters that could be detrimental and to neutralize all threats. The history of war is filled with the stories of men who risked life and limb to rescue, protect, and stand with their comrades in arms. Unparalleled bravery bursts forth in a man's conduct in now or never, do-or-die situations. When life is on the line, men most often do what only men can do—they exhibit incredible valor. It's as natural as breathing, buried deeply in the DNA of the Creator's design for manhood.

FIRED FROM MY JOB

I was a guard with Stinson Security in my hometown during college. At one point, Kathy was away at Bible college for a semester in Western Canada. I was a little nervous of such a beauty being around so many eligible men, so we talked by phone every night while I was at my security post. One winter night, when we were arguing about some insecurity I was feeling because she was so far away, my boss pulled up in his patrol car. Three or four times he tried to get me to hang up as I harangued my future wife on the phone. Each time I put him off with my index finger in the air and kept talking. Finally he left and I finished my call. The next day I was fired. I was being paid to watch the factory but rightfully lost my job because my own agenda intruded on the work I was hired to perform.

FIRST THINGS FIRST

What agenda is intruding on God's calling to be the watchman in your home? About what are you holding up your finger and dismissing your real job because you think something is more urgent than this? Nothing is more important than your family. Nothing comes before your responsibility to watch out for them and provide a home safe from any assault upon them, body or soul. The television programs watched in your home are your responsibility. Every site visited by a computer or smartphone in your house is on you. Keep watch! Who your kids' friends are, where they go when they are away from you is your responsibility. You're the watchman! How conflict is resolved, how Christ is prioritized, where the Word of God is positioned—all of it is entirely yours to oversee and you will answer to God for the job you did.

QUESTIONS FOR REFLECTION

1. Why is it so hard for men to stay focused on what matters most?

2. What is your biggest distraction from the priority of watching out for your family?

3. What are the biggest threats currently to God's best for your family and what can you do today to neutralize those threats?

4. How might reviewing your God-given role with family members help you do your job more effectively?

Prayer:

Father,
I shudder at the thought that an enemy of Your purposes would gain influence over my family on my watch. Please grant me courage as I recommit to this role You have ordained for me. Let me not fear a negative response as I insist on eliminating detrimental influences from the home You have called me to watch over. Grant me strength as I seek to be an example of

integrity and purity to my wife and children. Lead me and give me great wisdom as I make decisions about the protection of those I love most and help us all to love You more faithfully. In Jesus' great name, amen.

NEXT TIME:
WHO IS THE PATTERN FOR YOUR LIFE?

10

SNAP OUT OF IT!

If anyone does not provide for his relatives, and especially for members of his household, he has denied the faith and is worse than an unbeliever.[1]

"SNAP OUT OF IT!" Cher famously shouts as she slaps Nicolas Cage across the face in the 1987 blockbuster *Moonstruck*. She is not the first and certainly not the last woman to feel pretty dang frustrated with a man's seemingly infinite capacity to focus on almost anything except the few things that desperately need his attention. You would think that the more a man knows and loves God, the deeper he gets into understanding His Word, and the further he progresses in personal holiness, the better he would be at being a watchful man, but that is sadly not the case.

HOW IS THIS POSSIBLE?

I have a lot of favorite pastors, contemporary and historic, but my probable number one, a man I have studied in great detail, is actually another Chicago preacher. He had a great impact on the world for Christ but died when I was just three years old.

Aiden Wilson Tozer finished his ministry where mine began, in Ontario, Canada, but like me, spent multiple decades in one Chicago church; his an Alliance church on the South Side. I have heard numerous pastors state irrefutably that if they could have just two books other than their Bible, both would be from Tozer, and I tend to agree. *Knowledge of the Holy* and *The Pursuit of God* are absolutely life-altering books for hungry souls. I hope you will read them both. Tozer's sermons were fearlessly direct, passionately delivered, profoundly insightful, and precisely biblical. He was a student of culture as well as Scripture. He predicted fifty years ago much of the current malady of compromise and decay infecting the Western church today.

Tozer was not known to be a proud man, frequently expressing his own struggles and need for grace through his preaching and writing. How is it possible, then, that his fervent love for Christ did not seem to show up in his marriage or parenting? I really do not understand. Scripture is so clear that love for God must translate into love for those closest to us.[2] Neighbors are actually mentioned as the second priority because the Bible assumes you will not lose sight of your own family. But many men do. Even good godly men are failures where watchfulness is most needed and commanded. We see at the beginning of this selection what Paul told Timothy: that one who does not provide for his own family is **"worse than an unbeliever."** While provision certainly means a roof over their heads and food on the table, it cannot possibly exclude the soul care every family needs from its leader. **"For what will it profit a man if he gains the whole world, and loses his own . . ."**[3] [family]. I realize Jesus cautioned against losing **"his own soul,"** but what kind of man would prioritize his own life and see his family perish? Paul's compassion caused him to wish himself accursed for the sake of countrymen who were not family to him. Can we care less for our own flesh and blood?

Bestselling author Lyle Dorsett's excellent book *A Passion for God* details much that is commendable about Tozer's ministry and walk with the Lord, but also speaks candidly about his great contradiction. After his death, his widow remarried, and when asked about her happiness, Ada Cecelia Tozer Odam responded, "I have never been happier in my life. Aiden loved Jesus Christ, but Leonard Odam loves me."[4] Were this all we knew, we might conclude that Tozer wounded his wife early in a way that made his later efforts to love her well less effective but, "By early 1928 the Tozers had a routine. Aiden found his fulfillment in reading, preparing sermons, preaching, and weaving travel into his demanding and exciting schedule, while Ada learned to cope. She dutifully washed, ironed, cooked, and cared for the little ones, and developed the art of shoving her pain deep down inside. Most of the time she pretended there was no hurt, but when it erupted, she usually blamed herself for not being godly enough to conquer her longing for intimacy from an emotionally aloof husband."[5]

While not every marriage is a happy one, surely Tozer was more attentive to his seven children: "On and off over the years, Aiden exercised his role as head of the family by encouraging times of family devotions. These never lasted more than a few weeks. As one son explained, the children just did not want it and they were seldom all together for extended periods in any case."[6]

In reality, my greatest preacher was mostly a failure in his primary calling to be a husband and father. Waxing eloquent with great power and precision about the decline he saw in the culture and the church but unable to see the parallel decline in his own family. Watching but not watching at all, not where it mattered most. Why didn't someone take him by his mystical, isolationist shoulders and shout into his face, "Snap out of it!"?

URGENCY

I have chosen the word *urgency* to describe the state of a man's heart who is obeying the biblical imperative to act like a man and *watch*! Urgency means *fervent interest in high priority, intense attention to a matter of great importance.* I love that. Does urgency describe you in regard to your highest priorities as a man? Are you "on it" with urgency, watching your family, or are you asleep with your head elsewhere, even elsewhere good as with Tozer? Not even heavenly slumber will suffice as rationale before a holy God who has given you as a man responsibility for your family.

Romans 13:11 insists, **"Besides this you know the time, that the hour has come for you to wake from sleep. For salvation is nearer to**

us now than when we first believed." Salvation is a package deal that began in eternity past with God's sovereign act of election where He decided who He would save. Salvation launches for you personally at the moment of your repentance and faith. Salvation then continues through life as God sanctifies you bit by bit, conforming you to the likeness of His Son. Then salvation culminates when God brings this earth age to a close with His glorious return and transforms each of His saints in totality. In the verse above, Paul is saying in effect, "The final day is coming and it's a lot closer than it was when you first met the Lord. This is not a time to get lazy and snooze in the sunshine. Wake up, stay alert, pay attention, and live with urgency. Life is short; eternity is forever, seize your opportunities to lead and guide your home toward God's purposes, do it now!"

I LOVE THAT WORD

After thirty years in ministry, I have some truths that I treasure and love to repeat. One of those involves the etymology behind the word I used above, *opportunity*. It actually comes from two Latin words, *ob* and *porta*, meaning the perfect moment. The word was formed initially to describe what most of us landlubbers seldom get to see.

A few years back Kathy and I were speaking at a pastors' retreat in Scotland. As part of the trip we visited the city of St. Andrews and its seaport. Early in the afternoon, the docked ships are actually settled in the mud. Mired and motionless, it would take a crane to move the vessels even a few feet. But later in the day, when the tide is at its peak, those boats are lifted high by the ocean and could sail on their own anywhere in the world. That moment of high tide and maximum potential was called *ob-porta*, the premium opening—the time to seize with great urgency. Those who live away from the ocean have their own parallel phrase, "Make hay while the sun shines." Opportunities are seized by God's men with urgency. We recognize the chance to speak a word, take a stand, make a difference, carry a burden, and we take hold of it with urgency because we have been watching for that exact opportunity. **"Whatever your hand finds to do, do it with [all] your might."**[7]

QUESTIONS FOR REFLECTION

1. In all honesty, what has been the greatest urgency of your life in each decade—or every five years—since adolescence? Jot them down.

2. Describe the greatest moment of urgency in your life. How did you respond? Why?

3. What is it about our home life that seems to inoculate our urgency?

4. What can you do today to express your passion for your family and for God's agenda without alarming or overwhelming them?

Prayer:

Dear Father in heaven,
Thank You for being so passionate about my life for Your
glory even when I have been indifferent to You. Thank You for
bringing me closer and closer to Your heart and Your priorities.
Forgive me for the times I have allowed lesser things to conflict
with what matters most and lasts longest. Give me wisdom as
I seek today to bring greater urgency to Your agenda for my
marriage and family's future. Please continue this work in my life
so that I am daily being prepared for what You already know I
will face in the future with Your help. In Jesus' name, amen.

NEXT TIME:
HOW DO YOU HANDLE FOLLOWING DIRECTIONS?

11

MAN—DO I FEEL STUPID!

Keep a close watch on yourself . . . by so doing you will save both yourself and those who hear you.[1]

A MENTOR OF MINE ONCE SAID, "If you don't know where you are going, any road will take you, and you won't know when you get there." Good advice I got in the spring of 1981, but I really needed it in the fall of 1979. A recent high school grad, I was taking my dad up on his wise and watchful promise to offer his kids a free year of Bible college before university. For some reason my other siblings took a pass, but God had been working in my heart and though I was 100 percent certain, even determined, that I would not go into ministry, a year away was very attractive regardless of location. After about ten minutes of careful consideration, I settled on Tennessee Temple in Chattanooga, the alma mater of my youth pastor.

The budget was tight, so the planned transportation to my freshman year was a 1967 Dodge Dart that someone needed in Chattanooga. Mary, a former girlfriend, I had hardly seen since, got into the passenger seat for the same journey and off we went. Things were smooth as we crossed the border from Ontario to Detroit with our student visas. I had never driven outside Canada, and my anxious father followed up the send-off prayer with some final words: "When you get to Detroit, get on I-75. Don't stop 'til you get to Chattanooga!"

My nervousness grew as I entered a foreign country and scanned the roadside for the needed signage. Watching, watching like a hawk, I lunged at the first red, white, and blue sign reading I-75. It was already planned as a twelve-hour trip, three times longer than any one-day outing I had ever attempted, more than 750 miles. For that reason I was keeping my speed up, but after more than two hours of watching 1-75 signs race past, I noticed the signs had a little rectangle below: NORTH. Then I felt a growing pit in my stomach. Hadn't my father also said I would see Toledo exits within an hour of the border? But I hadn't seen any of those. With Bay City, Michigan, in my rearview mirror, my stubbornness gave way to sadness and I pulled off the highway in Linwood, Michigan, to turn around. Five hours after crossing the border, we made it back to Detroit with 625 miles still to travel and a never-to-be-forgotten awareness of the difference between north and south. This was before GPS and smartphones and before I had taken to heart the words, "If you don't know where you are going, any road will take you, and you won't know when you get there."

ESAU

Esau was on the wrong road too, but refused to see it. Grandson to Abraham, the patriarch of promise, Esau was born shortly before his twin, Jacob. Esau was a manly man to be sure. The Bible tells us he was hairy and a hunter, strong and certain in all he did. I see Esau in flannel with a gun over his shoulder and a beard down his chest, the kind of guy you like to watch a game with or fight a battle with—but God hated Esau. Malachi opened his prophetic book quoting the Lord's view of the man: **"I have loved Jacob but Esau I have hated."**[2] Both men had the same father and lineage, so why would God hate one and love the other?

The answer is found in Jacob's heart for the things of God and Esau's disdain for all things vertical. After an especially exhausting day in the forest hunting, Esau stomped in famished and demanded a sampling of the sumptuous stew Jacob had prepared. Jacob was both spiritually minded and shrewd, countering with a demand of his own as he held back the dripping bowl of gravy and meat. "Sell me your birthright," Jacob said, because he had always resented the firstborn status granted to his twin for being just a few minutes older. What was treasure for Jacob was trivia for his profane brother whom the book of Hebrews calls **"unholy like Esau, who sold his birthright for a single meal."**[3] Later Esau decided he wanted the birthright back, but couldn't sincerely repent because the things of God actually meant nothing to him. You won't see Esau in heaven. He refused, rebelled, and rejected the things of God to the point where it was too late for him. He never repented and eventually couldn't, because God, who grants repentance, didn't want him to. **"For you know that afterward, when he desired to inherit the blessing, he was rejected, for he found no chance to repent, though he sought it with tears."**[4]

IS IT EVER TOO LATE TO REPENT?

The answer to that is assuredly *yes*. In Genesis 6:3 (NKJV) God says, **"My Spirit shall not strive with man forever."** Popular today is the notion that you can sin, resist, refuse, and put off God and His grace at will until you are good and ready, but that is not the case. Esau kept putting God off and living a profane life until he came to the place where he couldn't get back. He pleaded, he cried, and even shed selfish tears, but he was not sincere and was rejected. The word for rejected there in Hebrews 12 is the Greek term *adokimos*, the scariest word in the New Testament, and no one is above concern that they could get there.

Paul himself lamented his own concern in 1 Corinthians 9:27 that **"after preaching to others I myself should be disqualified,"** or *adokimos*. The word means cut off, permanently separated from the life of God on earth and destined with no possibility of parole to an eternity in hell. Every Christian with biblical watchfulness knows the importance of **"work [ing] out your own salvation with fear and trembling."**[5] Good works save no one but they are the obvious and increasing evidence of a person genuinely saved. The Bible calls that evidence *fruit* and Jesus says in Matthew 7:20 (NKJV) it's the way we recognize each other **"by their fruits you will know them."** A farmer who plants a pear tree will soon tear it up by the roots if it does not bear fruit. And Jesus says in John 15:2, **"Every branch in me that does not bear fruit he takes away** (v. 6 says those sticks go into the fire, a clear reference to hell itself), **and every branch that does bear fruit he prunes, that it may bear more fruit."** All that to say this with biblical authority—you must wake up and live for Christ with urgent watchfulness while you still can, while you still care. If you don't, you will reach the point of refusal Esau reached and find out in the end, through your tears, that you never really had saving faith and tolerated your unbelief past the point of no return.

I felt so stupid as a first-day freshman when I discovered I had blindly barreled up that Michigan highway at breakneck speed in the wrong direction. But I did stop and suffer the shame of turning around and heading in the right direction. If you don't know where you are going, any road will take you, and you won't know when you get there. If you are on the wrong road, stop now and turn around. The first person you need to watch out for, the first urgency you need to attend to, before you ever get to your family, is yourself. **"Keep a close watch on yourself . . . by so doing you will save both yourself and those who hear you."**[6]

QUESTIONS FOR REFLECTION

1. What personal pattern of current behavior could rightly be labeled "wrong direction"?

2. Where will you end up if that pattern persists unbroken?

3. What blessing would flow to your life immediately if you repented of that sin and confessed it to a brother for accountability going forward?

4. Why have you waited so long to make this decision?

5. What prevents you now from turning to God in sincere repentance while you still can and while you still care?

Prayer:

Dear Father in heaven,
(write out your own prayer of repentance)

NEXT TIME:
ANOTHER LOOK AT PAUL AND ROUGH-CUT
GUYS LIKE HIM—AND MAYBE YOU

12

YOU'RE ONLY LYING TO YOURSELF

Do nothing from selfish ambition or conceit, but in humility count others more significant than yourselves.[1]

I AM SORRY; I HAVE JUST SEEN too much to be surprised anymore. Too often the loudest, most outspoken champion for truth, righter of wrongs, Bible doctrine watchdog, Internet troll, pseudo Christian superhero, blowhard is the guy with the filthy life.

I've seen it so much that it has softened my own rhetoric, scoured my heart for hypocrisy, and brought me to my knees begging God not to let me end up like that. The guy who discipled my sons in high school and had too much to say about my deficiencies as a dad (he wasn't wrong about me) has been unmasked as a serial adulterer in more recent times. He was run out of his job because the guys at the office got tired of barfing over his loud Jesus-talk while they watched him live like a pig. The guy who can't apologize, who always sounds off about how others are off base; the crusader from the pulpit, railing against every deficiency in town except the deterioration of his own church, reaching no one and ruled by self-righteousness. The flamethrowing activist launching tirades against every societal ill except the stream of sewage he privately saves on his own computer. These are the guys who make Joe Screwdriver hate Jesus and make it hard for us to win the lost around us. Petulant Pharisees, persistent to the max, they are filled with pride and sadly—apart from a grace awakening—doomed to perdition.

If you are like this, you better start running in the other direction because people who have been saved by grace grow to love giving grace to others. If you don't love more and better than you used to, you are just not saved. It's time you stopped lying to yourself. **"If anyone says, 'I love God,' and hates his brother, he is a liar."**[2]

I WANT TO MEET HIM MYSELF

I read it in Christian periodicals and across the blogosphere, I heard it in conversations and at conventions, and closer friends frequently asked me about it: "What do you think of Mark Driscoll? Why did he do this or that or . . . ?" Why was it that everywhere I turned, pastors and parishioners alike were teeing this guy up and driving his ministry and reputation down the middle of the fairway? Weary of the ways we put Christian leaders on a pedestal and then tear them down, I had to meet Mark Driscoll and form my own opinion. No way was I gonna keep taking my cues from guys who sniper fellow Christians and call murder-by-friendly-fire a ministry. It wouldn't have mattered much, except Mark was the most downloaded podcast among Bible preachers and a productive church planter through the Acts 29 network he founded. He also pastored one of the fastest growing churches in America that seemed to have cracked the code on how to stop shuffling believers from church to church and actually penetrate our lost culture with the good news of Jesus Christ. Mark had become infamous for crass language from the pulpit and frequent uncalled-for frankness in his preaching about sexuality, to name just a couple of the controversies.

When I reached him by phone, we agreed to meet the next time he was in Chicago, and soon we were slipping out of a conference meeting to take in a Cubs game. Hours of banter in the traffic jam, at the game, and on the way back to the hotel, we cemented a relationship. I took the opportunity, being ten years older, to exhort him in a few areas, and saw him respond with humility. Not once since that day have I seen him reverse course on what God was teaching him or ever take a backward step in his sanctification. Mark came from a broken, violent home and grew up far, far from Christ. He seems rough around the edges to the Christian subculture but what do we expect? He did go to seminary but started a nondenominational church to reach guys like himself. He's not some silver spoon, third-generation pastor who hasn't sat with a sinner in two decades, and thinks avoiding worldliness means being clueless about the culture while prudishly maintaining Victorian notions of purity. Mark and I prayed together when I dropped him off, and he said with a wink as he jumped out of my car, "I don't want to get matching sweatshirts or anything, but I think we can be friends."

That was several years ago, before we did relief work in Haiti and Japan, before we spoke in each other's churches and at a few other conferences. That was prior to meeting his wife and kids and long before I agreed to sit on his accountability board. We were friends before any of the many chances I have had to observe his immense humility, his tireless and resilient passion to serve Christ, and his staggering capacity to listen, learn, grow, and keep going. He watches out for his family and serves them with an urgency that is unsurpassed among the many Christian leaders I know. In our Act Like Men events, his message is a favorite for its fresh treatment of Scripture and compelling call for men to extend the chain of generational obedience to Christ within their own families. A real-life example of a man who is acting like a man.

PAUL WAS ROUGH AROUND THE EDGES

I can honestly say I think the "nice police" would run Paul out of most evangelical churches. By his own admission, Paul's speech was rough, his stature was unimpressive, and his presence was contemptible. In 1 Corinthians 4:10–13 Paul calls himself **"poorly dressed . . . homeless . . . reviled . . . slandered . . . like the scum of the world, the refuse of all things."** Paul used a graphic word for human excrement to describe his self-righteousness before Christ, and the Holy Spirit put that word in the Bible. Paul was too much for some, not enough for others, and clearly found comfort in the fact that God chooses the foolish of the world to confound the wise.[3]

Paul's biggest problem was that he was just a lot more fired up about serving Jesus than the politically correct who found him so over-the-top. Please hear me on this. Paul's delineation of elder characteristics in 1 Timothy 3 and Titus 1 were never intended as a pretext for self-righteous purveyors of pride to pronounce verdicts on the ministries of people they hardly know and have no right to condemn. The biblical qualifications of an elder were meant to provoke sober reflection among would-be church leaders and deliberate protection of the body by those already serving, who would select future leaders for that church. I have never met the man who meets every qualification without qualification, but I have met a few whose pride in asserting they did assured they did not.

The key character trait is first on both lists: **"above reproach."**[4] This does not mean that the man is perfect, or nobody would qualify. Above reproach does not mean he won't be attacked or criticized by anyone, anywhere. In practice, above reproach means that no accusation against an elder's character squares with the facts as understood by fellow elders in that church who have the authority to make that determination.

MY APPEAL

I appeal to you as my brother in Christ. If you are among the self-convened who slander people in ministry from the safety of the sideline, with partial facts and no standing in a local church, please stop immediately. You are hurting the cause of Christ, not helping. If a man must be removed from ministry, pray for the elders and appeal to them privately to act on the facts. If they fail to do their job, you can leave in quiet confidence that God will take action in the right measure, at the right time, but you have no right to launch your own holy war against the church of Christ. You are not better than others. You have no position of authority, let alone superiority and by acting as if you do, you are just lying to yourself.

The Bible commands, **"Be not wise in your own eyes,"**[5] and **"In humility count others more significant than yourselves."**[6] God's Word has nothing good to say about the critic, but it does commend the wise man who listens and learns from everyone, even loving his enemies. Let's do better at ignoring the noise of those who only seek to destroy, and let's continue to grow in grace and the knowledge of Jesus, seeking to serve Him with greater urgency every year, as long as He gives us breath.

QUESTIONS FOR REFLECTION

1. Do you find it hard to sit under your pastor without comparing him in a negative light to someone else?

2. Do you seek to be open-minded about Christians who prioritize different things about following Jesus than you do?

3. How do you think your actual holiness compares to the men who lead your church? Do you think you are better or worse at modeling Christlike behavior?

4. Jesus says that love for God and others is the summation of the Scriptures. In what ways are you growing in love that is apparent to those around you?

5. What could you do today to encourage your pastor or another leader in your church and help them carry the heavy load of shepherding Christ's church?

Prayer:

God,
I ask for a greater expression of humility in my interactions with others. I ask You to grow me in grace and remind me that Your "judgment is without mercy to one who has shown no mercy."[7]

Forgive me for asking others to measure up to a standard that I am not entirely fulfilling in my own heart. Please alert me immediately to thoughts of superiority that reveal a higher view of myself than of others. I ask You to make me an ambassador of Your mercy and lead me into loving interaction with others, which reveals my awareness that we all have a very long way to grow. Thank You for the grace of the gospel that assures my forgiveness in Christ; help me to extend that same forgiveness to others. For the fame of Jesus' name, amen.

NEXT TIME:
KNOWING WHO WANTS
TO DISTRACT YOUR URGENCY

13

HEADED FOR THE DITCH ON A SUNNY DAY

*The thief comes only to steal and kill
and destroy. I came that they
may have life and have it abundantly.[1]*

TAIL OF THE DRAGON IS A WINDING forest road where men die every year. Twisting through the west boundary of the Great Smoky Mountains National Park, it crosses the border between North Carolina and Tennessee. Tail of the Dragon is considered one of the premier motorcycle and sports car driving experiences in the world.

Take the plunge from the top and you will hit 318 hairpin curves packed into eleven miles of US 129 with an overall elevation change of a thousand feet. That's about twenty-nine curves per mile—a scary, sharp turn every sixty yards. An immensely exhilarating stretch of road, there are no intersections, no houses or driveways, and no businesses—just you and your vehicle going as fast as you dare through each unique curve, banked like a race track. More than 500,000 visitors a year come to Deal's Gap to see and maybe attempt a safe run down the Tail of the Dragon. Over the past decade, the injuries are too numerous to count but average to about three fatalities a year where someone lost control and went over the edge.

DOWN WE GO!

Imagine the pounding in my heart as I raced the engine of my Harley Road King and launched into steep turn #1 down the Tail of the Dragon. The ride lived up to its billing as an exhilarating, exhausting, exciting, adrenaline high to the max. I wish you had been there to see our joy when we got to the bottom, spent but satisfied and still sitting up. After some lunch, a quick picture, and souvenirs, we headed for a more relaxed part of our road trip. Early the next morning, with a big breakfast in our stomachs, we reached the Blue Ridge Parkway, which weaves lazily through the Smokies, just in time to see the morning sun burning up the mountain mist. Then, with the valley floor far below us, we stopped at a scenic lookout for another snapshot.

As the four Harleys pulled back onto the highway, my dear friend Kevn Dekker (who cofounded our broadcast ministry *Walk in the Word*) was leading the way. In a fraction of a second, as he checked his mirror to make sure we were in tow, his front wheel left the narrower pavement of the mountain road that had no shoulder and slipped deeper into the culvert. In that moment he had to decide whether to attempt to yank his front wheel back to the road, forcing a fall, or to ride it out and return to the road more gradually. He chose the latter. But the Harley bottomed out hard, forcing his feet in the air and up he went. Flipping forward in a terrible somersault, he came off the cycle and, as time froze, landed on the pavement with a bounce, facedown, and toward me. Screeching to a halt, I tore off my head gear and ran to my friend, who was motionless and unconscious. Kevn insists he wasn't knocked out, but generally speaking, the guy it happens to is less aware. After about twenty seconds he moved a bit and cried out in pain. Suffering a broken shoulder, fractured ribs, and a cracked collar bone, he was lucky to be alive, and we were very grateful for God's hand of protection over our friend.

Kevn is a highly skilled and experienced rider, much more than I am.

That's why he was leading the way. I have mentally replayed that awful scene countless times and still can't believe it happened so fast. How is it possible that he negotiated the Tail of the Dragon with ease and expertise but later lost control on a smooth stretch of straight roadway? In my experience, the crash happened where men crash most. Not on the hard road with all the twists and turns, but on the sunny day when all is well and they least expect to fall.

AN ANGEL OF LIGHT

God has given men a great leg up to victory and joy by revealing that our enemy Satan comes to us as an **"angel of light."**[2] You may be hearing from the devil when you least expect it. Since the garden of Eden, his approach has always been the same. First, he *disguises* himself. He draws your attention to an emptiness in your marriage or a lack of satisfaction in your work. He lies to you about what you really need to be satisfied or what you must have to experience a sense of accomplishment in your life. If you just bag that bear, make that sale, conquer that woman, or climb that mountain, then you will be fulfilled as a man. The thoughts he plants are always lies because Satan is **"a murderer from the beginning, and does not stand in the truth, because there is no truth in him. When he lies, he speaks out of his own character, for he is a liar and the father of lies."**[3] You think you're cruising in the sunshine when in reality you are heading into the ditch. Satan's moves are so pathetically consistent it's shameful we still get fooled.

Next, he *divides* you from the people you need most and love most deeply. C. S. Lewis in his book *Screwtape Letters* imagines an extended exchange of correspondence between a veteran demon and his apprentice known as Wormwood. In one of the letters instructing the younger demon, he exhorts:

My dear Wormwood,
Through this girl and her disgusting family the patient is now getting to know more Christians every day, and very intelligent Christians,

too. For a long time it will be quite impossible to remove spirituality from his life. Very well then; we must corrupt it. No doubt you have often practiced transforming yourself into an angel of light as a parade-ground exercise. Now is the time to do it in the face of the Enemy. The World and the Flesh have failed us; a third Power remains. And success of this third kin is the most glorious of all. A spoiled saint, a Pharisee, an inquisitor, or a magician, makes better sport in Hell than a mere common tyrant.[4]

For Satan's purposes, making you a completely ineffective and isolated follower of Jesus is as much a success as keeping you lost in sin.

Once he has the lie disguised as light and has divided you from those who can turn the light on for you, he moves in for the kill with his final move: destroy. Speaking of Satan, Jesus said in John 10:10, **"The thief comes only to steal and kill and destroy. I came that they may have life and have it abundantly."**

STRONGHOLDS ARE EVERYWHERE

Spend some time talking to men and you will find that the Enemy has captured a lot of ground in the battle over lies men believe. Even Christian men have too much satanic deception rolling around in their heads—lies my friend Pastor Eric Mason calls strongholds. Eric pastors Epiphany Fellowship in Philadelphia and speaks for our Act Like Men events, suggesting several satanic strongholds that exalt themselves against the knowledge of God in a man's mind.

- Truly fulfilling sexual practice cannot be found within monogamy = lie
- Passive avoidance of family issues will improve the problems over time = lie
- Avoiding deeper relationships with men conquers my fear of rejection = lie
- Past failure and hurt will fade into insignificance if ignored long enough = lie
- I can expect fidelity from my wife in body/mind even if I don't reciprocate = lie
- The church is weak and not the right place for a boy to learn to be a man = lie

This is just a sampling of the kind of strongholds men believe deeply and grip tightly. No matter how good things may be in your health or career or even at home, strongholds will take you down. If you are making decisions in isolation based upon the lies of the Enemy, you are headed for the ditch on a sunny day. I implore you to **"keep watch over yourself."**[5]

QUESTIONS FOR REFLECTION

1. Why is it essential that keeping a watch on your own life comes first?

2. What lies of the Enemy have you fallen prey to that need exposure to God's light?

3. In what ways has isolation from others made it tougher for you as a man?

4. Note the list above for any lies that have taken root in you. What can you do today to tear down strongholds of deception in your life?

5. Who do you know who needs this truth, and will you share it with him today?

Prayer:

Dear Father,
Thank You for exposing my heart today to the reality of our Enemy and his schemes. I see how I can easily fall prey to believing lies about myself and what is best for me and my family. Please grant me greater awareness to the angel of light and let me be alerted to his attempts to separate me from brothers who can be all You desire. Give me watchful eyes and listening ears to Satan's attack upon my family and let me apply

my greatest urgency to being a godly man for my family and for Your glory. Help me to walk in total dependence upon You throughout this day. In the name of Jesus Christ our Savior, amen.

NEXT TIME:
WHO'S IN YOUR CORNER
WHEN IT COMES TO URGENCY?

14

NEVER GIVE UP

I love the LORD, because he heard my voice and my pleas for mercy. Because he inclined his ear to me, therefore I will call on him as long as I live.[1]

IT IS THE CLOSEST I HAVE EVER come to running my vehicle into the ditch and I wasn't riding my Harley or heading down a winding road.

I was on a four-lane highway with light traffic close to my house and I had a widely regarded Christian leader on the phone. He had offered to pray for my broken heart over my prodigal daughter. Days of turmoil followed by nights of tossing and turning had left me pretty raw and I wept as I drove and leaned on this well-known pastor for hope in the midst of my deepest valley. I had been praying and pleading with the Lord but things were so bad with my only girl I couldn't even imagine a scenario whereby it could be different. My voice was hoarse from constant petition, day after day, asking for a God-sized miracle that seemed as impossible as asking the Lord to give me a third arm. So I was calling in some reinforcements for agreement in prayer and had dialed the man I thought had the full, backstage pass to God's throne room. If only he had just prayed in faith as we are commanded to.

Instead he said, "I will pray, but before I do I have to ask, have you considered the possibility that your daughter is just not one of God's elect?"

Wow, I gotta say his question put me in the ditch as I drove, figuratively and almost literally. "No," I said, "I haven't considered that and I won't. I know that the Lord is **'not willing that any should perish'**[2] and I've read **'believe on the Lord Jesus Christ, and you will be saved,** *you and your household.*'[3] I understand that Exodus 20:5–6 promises God's judgment to **'the fourth generation of those who hate** [Him], **but showing steadfast love to thousands of those who love** [Him] **and keep** [His] **commandments.'"**

A pretty awesome answer on the spur of the moment, right? Well it would have been, but I couldn't think that fast and simply said I didn't agree before he prayed his weak, faithless prayer and we hung up.

However in His sovereignty, God used a man preoccupied with this attribute to remind me that yes, He is sovereign. God is sovereign even over people who make His sovereignty into a reason *not* to pray in faith and believe that He is **"watching over my word to perform it."**[4] Don't emphasize any truth of Scripture to the exclusion of others, leaving your theological system airtight, without a single breath of mystery allowed in. This approach is doomed from the start. God is always infinitely larger than any of our descriptions of Him. I feel sorry for that man's kids if they ever need a watchful dad who will pray day and night until the work is done and the battle is won.

On the other hand this man's faithless readiness to blame God for not doing what He has told us He wants to do is not all that uncommon among men. Giving up is easier than going to war. But it is a long way from acting like a quality watchful man, and it wasn't the first time I had heard such folly.

FOUR GENERATIONS OF MACDONALDS

In an era of smartphones and constant photo taking, you probably have a truckload of family pictures like we do. Even before strangers stopped me weekly at church for a quick pic with the pastor, my wife was diligently preserving our family heritage in countless albums of creative memories. Of the thousands of pictures we have on file, there is one far above the rest that is my greatest treasure. It's a picture of me standing outside the little country Baptist church that I was born into and where I first heard the gospel. In the picture my brother and I are holding the hand of our great-grandfather, who was ninety at the time and I was just four. Moments before, I had my picture taken holding my great-grandfather's hand as my brother held my grandfather's hand on the other side and my dad (barely over thirty, now in his late seventies) leaned between his father and grandfather with his arms around their necks. Four generations of my family all worshiping Christ in the same church at the same time. Had they lived long enough, they would have seen my two sons and the son of one of my brothers as preachers and all of our kids following the Lord. I hope to see my grandsons preach the gospel and if I live as long as my great-grandfather, maybe I will hold a great-grandson's hand on the church steps after worship; that would be six generations. Is your head spinning? Do you see how important this is to me?

WHAT YOU BELIEVE AFFECTS HOW YOU PRAY

My grandfather Jack MacDonald did not believe in generational obedience to Christ. Saved as a young man under the ministry of a country preacher, my grandfather had one son and four daughters. When I became a man, my father told me that his dad had been taught by some faithless theologian (an oxymoron) that each successive generation in his family tree would walk farther and farther away from the faith. Sadly he grieved until his dying day what he believed was the inevitability of his kids not loving and serving Jesus. Thankfully, God sovereignly promoted him to heaven at seventy-two and left my godly grandmother to pray, weep, and plead to her dying day for the salvation of her five children and fifteen grandchildren, most of whom are now following the Lord. The idea that God, who loves the world and is not willing for any to perish, has irreversibly sealed hell as the destination of some of your kids should stir great anger in you. Using the precious and biblical doctrine of sovereign election to harbor the lie that God does not desire the salvation of successive generations of His children is a deceptive stronghold that must be torn down for the glory of His name. When theologians attempt to elevate what God says about His sovereignty above what He says about His desire to save, they promote passivity in God's men and destroy our desire to obey Christ's instruction that men **"ought always to pray and not lose heart."**[5]

PRODIGALS DO COME HOME BY GOD'S GRACE

In Isaiah 43:5–7 God promises, **"Fear not, for I am with you; I will bring your offspring from the east, and from the west I will gather you. I will say to the north, Give up, and to the south, Do not withhold; bring my sons from afar and my daughters from the end of the earth, everyone who is called by my name, whom I created for my glory, whom I formed and made."**

For many months I lived in the prophecies of Isaiah given to God's people so long ago but applicable to us today who long to see God move in saving power among the members of our families. I preached, prayed, fasted, and waited. I had always known what it was to kneel in prayer, but I learned what it is to see my tears fall on the carpet a few inches from my face many times. Then God answered, not all at once but so specifically and continually and miraculously that now I say, **"I love the LORD because he has heard my voice . . . because he inclined his ear to me, therefore I will call on him as long as I live."**[6] In those dark days I could never have dreamed my daughter would become one of the most authentic and compelling Christian women I know.

When I wrote a book about prodigals called *Come Home*, Abby wrote the foreword and we have told the story together with great rejoicing on *Walk in the Word*, our radio broadcast. Abby and I have the most glorious fellowship in prayer and following Jesus a father and daughter could ever hope for. Never, ever give up on your kids. Refuse the lie that God may not have planned for their participation in His kingdom. Pray and believe and keep waiting in unconditional love and stop listening to the "have nots because they ask nots."[7] Our highest calling is to our wife and kids. If you are serious about acting like a man, you won't stop until all whom the Father has given you are resting safely in His saving embrace. Refuse to see God's sovereignty as a barrier to your prayers; see it instead as the assurance that no matter how far those we love get from grace, sovereignty can find and bring them home. Work for it, watch for it, and wait for it by faith.

QUESTIONS FOR REFLECTION

1. Have you seen Mark Driscoll's sermon on generational obedience on the Act Like Men site? Check it out.

2. How many generations in your family have followed Christ before and after you?

3. How does your place in your family's generations of faith affect your viewpoint?

4. What is the hardest thing you have waited on God for and are you still praying?

5. God rejoices at the salvation of the lost. In what does your life evidence this joy?

Prayer:

Father,
I praise You for this call upon my life to greater urgency in what matters most to You. Please draw my attention today to people You are trying to reach. Please pursue me by Your grace about persisting in prayer for the salvation of those I love. Please raise generational obedience to Christ as the most urgent goal of my life and give me eyes to see where work is needed toward this lofty goal. Thank You for Your promises about prayer and

salvation, and give me faith to persevere until I see this work completed. In Jesus' wonderful name, amen.

NEXT TIME:

SEEING URGENCY IN THE LIFE OF JESUS

15

JESUS WAS FIRED UP

His disciples remembered that it was written, "Zeal for your house will consume me."[1]

FERNANDO ORTEGA IS A SMALLER MAN of apparent Hispanic descent with a handsome face and a warm smile whose family can trace back eight generations in New Mexico. Fernando is also an award-winning Christian artist whose songs stir affection for Jesus and whose melodies truly lift the soul. When he came to our church for the first time, I was a bit nervous to meet him as we often are when being introduced to someone so greatly used of the Lord in our lives.

I remember where he was standing near the entry to our original campus in a warehouse. It would have been nice if someone had warned me, because I get pretty excited when I'm nervous and I kinda scared the little guy when I slapped him on the back and said, "Dude! Are you fired up to be here? We are so fired up you are here! Are you fired up to be here, Fernando?"

I will never forget his startled look and soft voiced, slow reply, "Well, I'm not really a fired-up kind of guy."

"Well," I said, "I'm fired up enough for both of us and we are really fired up you are here!" I think he thought I was an idiot. Good thing we became friends and did a lot of ministry events together, because I really love the guy. And guess what—he shows it differently; he doesn't shout or spit, but his love for Christ and serving His kingdom is just as urgent as mine is, though he demonstrates it in different ways. Now every time I see Fernando, he looks at me through his charming grin and with a twinkle in his eye says, "Hey, James, are you fired up?"

HOW ABOUT YOU?

Are you fired up about the things of God? Does an urgent passion burn in your heart to see God's purposes advanced in your life and through you, to others? Are you fired up and watching to see that phrase in the Lord's prayer answered before your eyes: **"your kingdom come, your will be done, on earth as it is in heaven"**?[2] They say a group takes on the characteristics of its leaders. That causes me some fear as I think about my family and the church I have pastored most of my life. I am sure my weaknesses are obvious to all, but I do take comfort in this: the men of our church are fired up. I often say I couldn't get ten men to come by the church at three in the afternoon to pick lint off the carpet, but I can and do get thousands of men to show up with passion for late-night prayer sessions. The men of Harvest Bible Chapel and the more than a hundred churches we have been blessed to plant are for the most part men with an urgent, on-fire faith that can take a hill on a rainy day, pay a price when the war is raging, and stand with fierce loyalty at all times for our brothers in Christ.

Let me ask you again, are you fired up about the Lord?

JESUS WAS FIRED UP!

I get so sick of distorted pictures of Jesus foisted upon us by people who seem to forget that a single snapshot of anyone can quickly become a caricature. Without question Jesus was gentle and kind. He was patient and compassionate beyond measure with a tender heart toward anyone suffering in sin or shame. But Jesus was not weak. Down with that soft-palmed, hollow-forehead, weak Jesus who couldn't hold His own in a shouting match, let alone lay someone out who threatened His mother. That is not the Christ of the Bible. He is a man's man who would be just as comfortable talking to dudes at the NRA convention as He would be in line at the bank or across from you on the commuter train. He was loved by all, except religious hypocrites (who sadly seem to have the loudest voice in our day about who Christ was and is).

Jesus is strong and masculine in every righteous way that word can be used. And He didn't need to act like a man, He created man[3] and became a man[4] to reconcile all things to Himself.[5] If you were at a party, a game, or at the beach, Jesus would be turning heads and drawing listeners just as surely as He did two thousand years ago. He was the furthest thing from a wimp, and if you could meet Him face-to-face today, you would look down first; in fact we would both look down immediately.

- Jesus made a whip out of cords to drive a bunch of charlatans out of God's house and nobody dared to stop Him.[6]
- Jesus stood up for an adulteress and stopped a crowd of people ready to stone her.[7]
- Jesus walked to the disciples on water in a storm and stilled it with the sound of His voice.[8]
- Jesus called the denominational leaders vipers to their face, telling them they were hell-bound, publicly accusing them of murder; and they were too afraid to do anything about it.[9]
- When the mob called out for Jesus' death, a **band of soldiers and some officers**[10] were sent to arrest Him because past attempts with smaller numbers had failed.

When we meet Jesus in the last book in the Bible, we learn He will be riding a white stallion, wearing a robe dipped in blood, wielding a sword with fire coming out of His eyes. Oh yeah, Jesus is fired up about everything that matters and wants His men to have the same urgency.

Do you?

URGENCY IS FOCUSED ON THE GOAL

Each gospel writer reveals the strength and passion of Jesus Christ from his own perspective, but Luke and John seem especially to show His urgent, watchful focus.

Yes, the miracles substantiated His deity and yes, the manner showed us how to live, but the primary focus of Christ's incarnation was His atoning death as payment for our sin. In John's gospel, everything Jesus did was in reference to "that hour." In John 2:4 He told His mother, **"My hour has not yet come."** In John 5:28 Jesus told the crowds that an hour would come when **"all who are in the tombs will hear his voice."**

In John 7:30 they wanted to arrest Him, **"but no one laid a hand on him, because his hour had not yet come."** In John 12:23 Jesus declared that the hour **"has come for the Son of Man to be glorified."** And then declared in John 12:27 that He would not ask to be saved from the hour because **"for this purpose I have come to this hour."** John 13:1 tells us **"Jesus knew that his hour had come."** Four times in John 16 alone, He references this "hour" of suffering. From His first conscious moment, Jesus knew He was born to die and rise again. Nothing in His life was random and His death was always His focused purpose. In John 10:18 He said, **"No one takes** [my life] **from me, but I lay it down of my own accord."**

ARE WE LIKE JESUS?

How seldom do we hear the call to Christlikeness include His intense, passionate focus on accomplishing the mission He came to fulfill. Lazy as we often are, we prefer "chill Jesus," who was great at a patio party but never seemed to have much of anything He had to get done. Again, this is an immense distortion of the biblical portrayal of the Lord. Ever patient with the hurting and downtrodden, Jesus didn't have time for religious blockheads and dudes who were into abusing women, kids, and the system to meet their selfish interests.

Count on this: if Jesus came to my men's group or visited your Sunday school class, people wouldn't doze off, check their phones, or return emails while He was talking. Nobody would set Him straight or tear into Him about world hunger or complain that inflation is on the rise. If Jesus Christ appeared before you right now, you would be on your face asking for mercy, and if you looked to the left or right, you'd see me there right beside you.

As men, we are not even in the ballpark of Christlikeness if we are not seeking to live with the focused urgency toward our mission the way He lived toward His.

QUESTIONS FOR REFLECTION

1. About what do you feel the greatest urgency? How does the Lord view that priority?

2. Can you think of a time you wasted big energy on stuff that didn't matter?

3. What do you struggle to ignore that steals your focus and quenches your fire?

4. What is your favorite biblical account of Jesus' intensity? Why?

5. When have you best expressed urgency about things that matter and, looking back, how did you feel about that?

Prayer:

Dear God,
Thank You for sending Your Son, Jesus, who modeled for me what perfect masculinity looks like. Forgive me for the times I have spent myself for what does not satisfy Your purpose in my life. Grant to me a greater focus on the urgent responsibilities You have given to me in my family and service to Your kingdom.

I pray for a fresh joy in serving You and an increased capacity to devote myself to the things that matter most. Thank You for the work You are doing in my life through this study. For Jesus' sake, amen.

NEXT TIME:
URGENCY COMES HOME

16

WATCHFUL HOME IMPROVEMENT

The fear of the LORD is the beginning of wisdom.[1]

THE GREAT NEED IN OUR WORLD today is quality men applying themselves to God's purposes with urgency. All around us are the ground zero disasters that happened because when the man was needed, he wasn't watching and didn't act like a man. In just the past week I talked to a man who described with passive resignation the total defiance of his eighth grade son who was out of control. "What are you gonna do?" I asked.

"We have tried everything," he said.

But when I probed, "everything" turned out to mean "everything that doesn't make things a lot harder for me." If you discover your child is battling you because their attitude is shaped by things they learned on the Internet, you can solve that with a phone call to cancel service or a sledgehammer to the screen, but either way it should not be a problem tomorrow. That doesn't mean you don't talk to them, reason with them, win them if you can to your viewpoint, etc. It just means that the unpopularity of an obviously right action should not hinder the execution of an obviously right decision.

My father is phlegmatic by personality and rational rather than emotional in his mode of decision making, but he broke out of that mold quickly when a situation called for urgent action. He applied corporal discipline when we were young, then later, lectures with consequences that made my adolescent heart yearn for the easier days of "spank and it's over." My dad, Verne MacDonald, was a farmer's son who chose elementary education as his career. Through the years he had some epic stories of kids who were impossible to educate and nearly as tough to manage. I remember his telling the story of a 6 foot 4 late 1960s eighth grader named Bill. My dad, topping out at 5 foot 8 in those days and maybe 170 pounds, had the difficult task of reining in this would-be assailant and many times having to give him the strap in the principal's office. Refusing the obvious intimidation of this juvenile delinquent, my dad stood his ground and won the kid over through firm discipline founded on his philosophy of tough love. He would often say that the only way to lead a classroom and manage difficult kids was to follow this protocol: "If they hate you in the fall, they will respect you in the winter and love you in the spring."

PARENTING 101

Sadly, most parenting today follows the protocol: if I can sit and reason with my toddler and help him understand why running in the street without looking both ways is dangerous, that is the best form of training. The problems with that approach are twofold: (1) it doesn't work, (2) it's not how God trains His children. Years later we ran into Big Bill around town. I saw my dad stiffen up as his former student approached and waved away the hand Dad offered, choosing instead to embrace my father and almost tearfully thank him for the impact Dad's courageous strength had on this boy, now a man.

Men act like men at home when they realize they will be held responsible for how well they represented God to their family. Training your children is commanded by Him and it must be age appropriate. **"By mere words a servant is not disciplined, for though he understands, he will not respond."**[2] Pain is a powerful teacher. So much so that God has woven pain into the fabric of every sinful action. We always say, "choose to sin, choose to suffer." And because God loves us, He ensures that all human behavior works that way. It's Dad's job to drive home the lesson. Doing right leads to blessing as surely as doing wrong leads to pain.

Fatherly training is artificial application of amplified consequences before the actions are big enough to scar their life. Why does Johnny get spanked for not picking up his blocks? If he's told to do it, and he refuses to do it, it's no longer a matter of blocks but of the will. And loving parental training will apply and amplify the consequences of Billy's wrong choices before those choices are big enough to scar him for life. That's the whole job right there.

Will he be angry that his will was challenged and defeated? Expect it. He needs you not to cave. Because if you cave, what will happen when he does that in high school, in college, or with a police officer?

A wise family trains their children in expectation of further life challenges. If you catch your child lying at age seven, it's a big deal. Effective parenting recognizes that a lie is a seed to a tree that can devastate your kids for a lifetime. So you get on it big-time. You make the consequences bigger, the application clearer, and the pain significant. You make this whole big thing out of this little thing. Why? Because you want your kids to learn when the stakes are small so they don't have to learn when the stakes are big enough to leave lasting damage.

I realize you may have never gotten wise discipline from your parents. Instead, you are having to learn in adulthood and bear the scars for a lifetime of selfish parenting that would not teach you big lessons when the stakes were small. Now, if being in Christ is anything, it's breaking the chain of failure. What your parents and grandparents didn't get done, you're going to get done for your kids.

TOOL TIME

There are four discipline tools in the hand of every parent to be used in varying degrees depending on their age.

- **The Rod.** You have the rod (spanking), which is only for rebellion, deliberate disobedience, or for lying, never for mistakes or immaturity.

How do you spank? Never in anger. You separate the child and explain to them what they did wrong. You spank them and then immediately restore them to fellowship. Don't leave them in a room for an hour. God doesn't do that. He never leaves us or forsakes us. Between two years old and five years old, spanking is used as needed, perhaps frequently.

• **Reproof.** The tool that takes over from the rod is reproof, a strong rebuke. Once they realize you never make warnings about spanking you are not willing to calmly carry out, you find it less necessary. Reproof is in the face, deep voice, intense, ominous, and fear-producing. "Don't do that again or else." And you better come up with "or else" if you get pressed.

• **Loss of Freedom.** The third tool in the hands of every parent committed to training their kids is the removal of freedom. The loss of privileges can make a deep impression particularly as children get older.

• **Responsibilities.** As the first three tools are doing their work, don't overlook the importance of giving children responsibilities in the home. Even young children can contribute helpfully to family life, setting the table, taking out trash. Work can also be part of punishment when you assign them extra duties as a consequence for poorly used freedom.

In using these tools you will not have produced a perfect child; you will have raised a person who can respond in a good way when they are wrong without rebellion, resistance, or deflection.

As a father, you are patterning your discipline after your heavenly Father, whom your children need to realize you deeply respect and love. God trains His children on a foundation of fear and later, perfect love casts out the fear. Because God is absolutely perfect and awesome, His parenting is free from errors. We know we can't say the same for ours. It's important that your kids know you know you're not perfect. One of the best ways to show them is when you admit you're wrong or ask them for forgiveness. Don't break trust with your kids by failing to admit failures. They see when you've blown it and it actually improves your standing with them if you're transparent. You love your kids when they screw up and admit it; they'll love you when you do the same.

The church and culture are crowded with parents who so want, even need their kids' love, that they can't give them the necessary discipline. Hebrews 12:5–11 makes the point that discipline is proof of love. And, shockingly, kids themselves understand this principle. I wish more parents did.

God knows whether you are passive, prideful, or humble in regard to your parental training of your children. Psalm 127:1 says, **"Unless the LORD builds the house, those who build it labor in vain."** Develop an alert and watchful humility that consistently follows God's pattern of discipline. But know that's not going to be enough. Absolutely depend on the Lord to work in the lives of your kids.

At this moment I'm counting on the Holy Spirit to drive home the truth you have just been reading. From the moment they are born, you have a limited opportunity to impact your kids for eternity—don't miss those times. Ask the Lord by His Spirit to give you the kind of urgency that allows you to take moments with your children to teach and lead them beyond discipline. Let them see how and why you fear the Lord and lead them to do the same.

QUESTIONS FOR REFLECTION

1. Would you say your discipline style is a repetition of how you were raised, the intentional opposite of your parents, or something else?

2. How are you and your spouse working out your differences in discipline style? Do the kids see a united or divided front?

3. Which of the four discipline tools described above fits most closely to the growth phase of each of your children? How are you using those tools?

4. How can you as a dad step up to greater involvement in your children's training?

5. What's the clearest point of discipline between you and your heavenly Father right now?

Prayer:

My Father in heaven,
Because Your name is holy, I want to acknowledge first how unworthy I am to even accept the title of father in my children's lives. I recognize that I fall painfully short of showing Your character to them. But I long to point them to You. Please keep me from doing or saying anything that would become a barrier between my children and You. But even more, please help me to be a dad who trains, guides, and loves my kids as You do. Teach me to reflect the same hard and soft combination of authentic love toward them that I am continually discovering in my relationship with You. In Jesus' name, amen.

NEXT TIME:
WE WILL BEGIN TO SEE HOW CLARITY
ALLOWS US TO ACT LIKE MEN

STAND FIRM

IN THE FAITH

17

URGENTLY UNCLEAR

Stand firm in the faith.[1]

I HAVE HAD A PASSIONATE LOVE RELATIONSHIP with fishing my whole life. As a kid I rode around the cottage lake in my granddad's boat, watching him and my uncles troll for fish with various lures, catching a lot of crud off the bottom but seldom seeing any fish. My dad's dad had a farm with some stocked ponds, and as a teen I would often sneak down and throw a line in the water without my grandma knowing, because she loved the trees and wildlife a little bit more than she loved us. It was fun to reel in a few quick catches, but it didn't seem legit to pull fish out of a stocked pond that was so thick with bass they would fight to bite a hook with no bait.

Patience has never been my best thing, so I always looked at fishing as both fun and sanctifying for me. For years I took every chance I got to go fishing in the "wild." From the world record steelheads in the Muskegon River by our church camp during the fall run, to fly-fishing off the coast of Alaska after preaching at a radio rally in Anchorage, and marlin fishing with church buddies in Costa Rica, I love the thrill of the catch and get real fired up when the sun rises on a day of fishing.

Imagine my excitement when a friend invited me to catch bass at a lake in Branson, Missouri. The guide was a Bass Pro Shop fisherman famous for his training videos and frequently seen on ESPN, but I can't give you his name for reasons that will be clear in a moment. Down to the dock and into the sleekest bass boat I have ever seen, covered in sponsor decals and equipped to the max with state-of-the-art fish finders, etc. The pro wasn't superfriendly—just another gig for him, I guess. We told him how excited we were to spend a day on the lake with an icon of professional bass fishing. He just grunted and told us to sit down.

The engine ignited with precision and obvious power, and we sped onto the lake toward some undisclosed secret location where the biggest bass no doubt were hiding. I was in the middle of the boat with my friend in the bow. When the engine cut, my heart was pounding and I knew I would tie into a ten-pound largemouth in moments.

The pro told us where to cast and what to do and I rose to my feet, feverish with anticipation. I drew back with my right hand, bail open, finger on the line, and cast with all my might to reach the farthest point for the biggest catch. I immediately heard a guttural scream from the back of the boat that could only be coming from the bass pro. Then I saw that his hat was attached to my lure and dropping gently to the water at the end of my line. Apparently my mighty cast had torn the hat from his head, hopefully without too much scalp.

I can't tell you everything he said next. The first reprintable word, after the string of adjectives, was "idiot," and I sure felt like one. How could I be so stupid? My face was flushed, my head held in shame, so much that I don't remember if we even caught any bass. The valued memory of that day was all eclipsed in the moment I made the superstar bass fisherman want to gut me with his filet knife. I was definitely fired up, but without focus I ended up feeling pretty foolish.

ALL DRESSED UP AND NOWHERE TO GO

Most men relate to the feeling of having more energy/passion than they know what to do with. It wasn't enough to be fired up about healthy fun like bass fishing; I needed to channel my urgency into a manner of expression that advanced rather than hindered my goal. In the last session we studied in detail how quality men watch over their families with great urgency. The problem is when our urgency is directed toward the wrong stuff or even directed toward the right people and issues but in the wrong amounts, in the wrong way, at the wrong time.

During my kids' adolescence it was tough for me to recognize and finally accept that my passion to see their lives on track with God's plan was not wrong but at times got expressed in ways that not only failed to help but at times actually made things worse.

In Proverbs we're warned that **"an angry man stirs up strife."**[2] Specific scenes of angry insistence upon God's will for one of my kids are etched in my memory not as courageous stands for truth, but at times I was actually hindering, through my lack of focus, what God was trying to accomplish. Passion is good, but it needs some parameters to keep it constructive versus destructive in the lives of those we love and are called to lead.

GET YOUR CLEATS IN THE TURF

In our theme verse for this book, 1 Corinthians 16:13–14, one of the five imperatives, the one that follows the call to be watchful, is **"stand firm in the faith."** This directive is there to focus the urgency God has given to men so that it will be directed toward things that matter and used in a way that partners with what God is trying to accomplish. Just as a lineman in football will dig his cleated toe into the turf to leverage his forward momentum once the ball is snapped, so the phrase "stand firm in the faith" leverages our watchful urgency over those we love.

Note there is a location for standing firm—*in the faith*. Paul doesn't just mean your personal trust in God at this point; he means faith as the body of truth that has been entrusted to us in the Word of God. Later he wrote to Timothy these summary words of his life: **"I have fought the good fight, I have finished the race, I have kept *the faith*."**[3] Paul understood that alongside the Old Testament Scriptures, God's Spirit had inspired, even through him, an added but limited revelation for the church going forward. He urged Timothy, **"By the Holy Spirit who dwells within us, guard the good deposit entrusted to you."**[4]

When Jude said, **"I found it necessary to write appealing to you to contend for *the faith* that was once for all delivered to the saints,"**[5] he was calling men to fight for what is true, to stand for what has been revealed in the Bible. He was talking about the body of truth that now has been passed down through the centuries recorded in God's Word.

What a man believes about God is the most important thing about him. You can't just make it up. If you are struggling to believe, struggling to persevere, struggling to carry the heavy weight that God puts on many men's shoulders, you need strong biblical theology. Someone has said that we pray for easier paths when we ought to pray for stronger shoes, and the stronger shoes of the Christian life are robust, biblical theology. Your success to act like a man will be a product of how well you really know God's Word. When the verses talk about *the faith*, they are referring to all God has provided for us in His Word.

Standing firm, when it comes to the faith, means holding the biblical ground without compromise. It is active, not passive—not leaning or sitting or retreating but standing. This is military language that calls to mind events like the Alamo, or Thermopylae, the last stand by the Spartans told in the movie *300*. It's about having a band of brothers you know stand with you. Paul is talking about protecting it, no matter how daunting the opposition. Stand for it, no matter how much it takes, and don't try to do it alone. We need men who understand that in failing to stand together for the faith as it has been entrusted to us, we are doing grave damage to the next generation.

QUESTIONS FOR REFLECTION

1. If you had to explain *the faith* to a friend or to one of your children, how would you begin, and what would you include?

2. When you think of *the faith* as you understand it at this point, what do you find difficult to stand for?

3. What does standing firm look like in your life right now and where could God and other men help you improve?

Prayer:

O Father in heaven,
I admit I am sometimes intimidated by Your Word. But I want
to be among those who stand for it and base their lives on
it. Help me not to use my lack of knowledge as an excuse
for failing to pursue more. Keep me from confidence in what
I know but increasing confidence in what You have said in
Scripture. Remind me that it remains true even when I don't yet
understand it. Draw me by Your Spirit into continued faithful
study of Your Word that I may be able to not only stand firm but
also share with my family how the Bible is making a difference
in my life. Guide me into the truth. In Jesus' name, the Way, the
Truth, the Life, I pray, amen.

NEXT TIME:
YOU CAN'T REALLY GET BY WITHOUT CLARITY

18

A CRAVING FOR CLARITY

Your words were found, and I ate them, and your words became to me a joy and the delight of my heart, for I am called by your name, O LORD, God of hosts.[1]

"Are we clear?"

"Crystal!"

"You want answers?"

"I want the truth."

"You can't handle the truth!"

I'M GUESSING YOU RECOGNIZE these most famous of movie lines, from the courtroom scene between Tom Cruise and Jack Nicholson in *A Few Good Men*. It is one of the most recognizable scenes of all time, and a favorite of all kinds of men. Two men with incredible urgency, both convinced of the priority of competing missions, each defending until the end what they decided to give their lives to, but both cannot be right. As Colonel Jessup is escorted away by the MPs, presumably to spend many years in prison, we learn again that urgency alone is not enough. There has to be clarity guiding our urgency so we spend our passion on the few things that truly matter.

CLARITY IS ESSENTIAL

From painted chests at football games and weekend civil war reenactments, to sixty-plus-hour weeks at work making widgets and walls filled with deer trophies, men are searching desperately for something that will engage their passion. As men we were fashioned by the Creator to spend ourselves for a worthy cause. Five centuries ago we would have been fighting to protect our city from invasion. Two hundred years back we battled the elements, tilling the soil and killing our own meat to provide for our family. With industrialization came the systemization and mechanization of life's necessities. This removed men from being generalists at a variety of functions that engaged us mind and body in significant survival challenges. Most men now screw a bolt, man a desk, or sell a something over and over and over, ad nauseam, and emerge from their work time with a ton of pent-up urgency. Sebastian Klein notes,

> The theory that following your passion leads to success first surfaced in the '70s, and in the intervening decades it's taken on the character of indisputable fact. The catch? Most people's passions have little connection to work or education, meaning passionate skiers, model railroaders, or stamp collectors run into problems. In a culture that tells people to transform their passions into lucrative careers, it's no wonder so much of today's workforce suffers from endless job swapping and professional discontent.[2]

That has also led to the spectacle of endless mental escapes in leisure that mostly involve beer and only heighten the frustration of not having anything meaningful to engage with.

PROMISES, PROMISES

I spent the nineties living in Chicago during the rise of Michael Jordan and the Chicago Bulls, who won six NBA championships in the greatest sports dynasty of the modern era. I was in the old stadium when they won the first one and at the United Center for the fourth. I watched Michael dance down the scorer's table with the trophy held over his head after championship number one. I was five hundred feet away when he crumpled on the floor in tears as pent-up grief over the murder of his father poured out of him like a river after number four. In fact, in an unbelievable anomaly, we stayed in our seats till the new stadium was almost empty and saw Michael, apparently cutting through to avoid the mayhem and get back to the locker room after his press conference. We ran over a few seats to the exit from the floor and his Airness high-fived Kathy and me as he ran out.

Here is what we all know too well. Victory is hollow. I enjoyed cheering for the Bulls' six rings and went out of my way to be in Philly back in 2010 when the Blackhawks won their first Stanley Cup in fifty years. However, the joy of any victory is a temporary high that doesn't last or maybe even make it to the end of that week. I have often reflected on how much more painful that realization would be if being a Chicago sports fan was my life, as it is to so many men. It's what they live for, wait for, drink for, even breathe for. It's what they talk about, argue about, and if you have been in the street or local bar after a game, fight about.

Much of the anger and relational dysfunction men exhibit is the overflow of despair they feel when they live for a result, expecting the fulfillment it promises, but have those hopes dashed. It's pretty tough to stand on the mountain and find the victory to be far less than you expected and really just another momentary rush.

Sports is just one example of men getting the urgency thing right but lacking clarity. Yes urgent, but urgent about things that matter and outcomes that will last. Most of what men pursue provides neither. For that reason, the Holy Spirit inspired Paul to include a call to clarity as a qualifier on the call to urgency. First Corinthians 16:13 calls us, yes, to **"be watchful,"** but then quickly adds, **"stand firm in the faith."** That is a call to clarity about our urgency. We are not acting like men until our urgency is engaged with full biblical clarity.

The last time, we looked at *the faith*, but I didn't try to boil it down much. I wanted you to recognize the importance of the Bible as the ultimate guide and explanation of faith. You needed to begin with the big picture of God's written revelation. I want to be as clear as I can possibly be here. God's Word doesn't change, the message doesn't shift. It can't be compromised in any way. It's where we stand firm.

FIVE GOSPEL WORDS

One of the great blessings of twenty-five years of ministry in the same city is my relationship with other pastors. For more than a decade, I met with an arbitrary list of some of the pastors of larger churches throughout Chicagoland; we met quarterly across racial, denominational, economic, across every line that separates people, gathering together around our common love for the gospel and the church of Jesus Christ. The experience was life-changing to me. One of the friendships that emerged from that fellowship was my relationship with Bill Hybels, who was from a very different background and who pastored a very different style of church. He was a good man and often wrongly maligned.

I will never forget the day Bill told the other pastors he was wrestling with how to hold the staff of his large church accountable for the essential elements of the gospel message. He challenged each of us to come up with five words that best summarized the gospel. What words are so essential that, if one of them is left out, at the end the person isn't even saved. Each word has to be included. To reduce it any further would be to go beyond the irreducible minimum. But if you don't have these five things, you don't have biblical faith. Paul instructed us to **"examine yourselves, to see whether you are in the faith."**[3] Remember, it's not "stand firm *for* the faith" but "stand firm *in* the faith." You've got to own it and live it.

These are the five gospel "gotta haves": God, sin, substitution, belief, and life. We have already touched on them in these studies and will return to them often.

God is a summary term for the Trinity as revealed in Scripture. The Father, the Son, and the Holy Spirit are one. **"And I [Jesus] will ask the Father, and he will give you another Helper, to be with you forever, even the Spirit of truth, whom the world cannot receive, because it** neither sees him nor knows him. You know him, for he dwells with you and will be in you."[4]

Sin is our universal condition of separation from God. We're born as sinners, **"for all have sinned and fall short of the glory of God,"**[5] already candidates for God's eternal judgment.

Substitution refers to what God did in Christ and His cross to rescue us from sin. He took our place and our punishment as our perfect Substitute. **"And you, who were dead in your trespasses and the uncircumcision of your flesh, God made alive together with him, having forgiven us all our trespasses, by canceling the record of debt that stood against us with its legal demands. This he set aside, nailing it to the cross."**[6]

Belief is placing our whole trust in Christ alone for forgiveness and eternal life.[7] Once we believe, we can stand firm in the faith.

Life is the present and future promise God gives to those who place their faith in His Son. **"I came that they may have life and have it abundantly."**[8]

It should never be an easy thing for a man to bring his family to a church where the true message is not front and center all the time. Most of us live on table scraps as it is, and church has to be an earth-shattering, window-rattling, and life-altering encounter with the God of the universe. I wrote about this extensively in my book *Vertical Church*. Standing firm in the faith means that just as you wouldn't take your family to a fast-food restaurant every night for dinner or let your children eat out of the neighbor's trash bin, you should never expose your family to a ministry that isn't foundationally committed to the authority of God's Word without apology.

QUESTIONS FOR REFLECTION

1. What are three locations/relationships where you realize you must intentionally stand firm in the faith? How is that going?

2. In what areas (start with the five gospel words) do you sense the need for greater clarity? Where and how are you going to get it?

3. Who are your role models for standing firm in the faith? How are you organizing your life to spend time with those men?

Prayer:

Father,
Thank You for showing me the connection between the five gospel words and the way each applies to me. Keep reminding me that standing firm isn't about my strength but Your power at work in me. Guide me as I seek to be clear on what You want me to understand and pass on to my family. I want to be a good example of trusting You even as I teach my children to trust You. In Jesus' name I pray, amen.

NEXT TIME:
WHERE'S CLARITY WHEN THE WORLD CAVES IN?

19

CLARITY IN CRISIS

The end of the matter; all has been heard.
Fear God and keep his commandments,
for this is the whole duty of man.[1]

I HEAR IT ALL THE TIME: Can't you just be positive? Why do you have to use negative examples? Isn't it better just to look for the good and stay upbeat at all times? Answer: no. This answer was brought to you by the all-time bestseller authored by the Holy Spirit Himself—the Bible.

While the culture is constantly focused on fluff and positivity, God's Word offers not just a competing worldview but a contrary one. The Bible is not some retouched photo of the human condition, sanitized to save everyone the heartache of reality. The Bible brings far more than a smiley preacher with platitudes that fade before sunset. The Scriptures bring stark reality, the depravity of the human heart apart from God. His Word declares the dangers of sin using the lives of men and women who needed a front-row seat to learn that all sin brings suffering. These real people are not presented to us as perfect but as those whom God was working on.

Yes, Christ sets us free from the *penalty* of sin through faith in Him, and yes, the *power* of sin is broken through salvation so we are no longer slaves to the flesh, walking according to the will of flesh. But the *presence* of sin is not broken yet and God wants it to be neutralized through our moment-by-moment relationship with Him. In practice, this means, **"Likewise you also, reckon yourselves to be dead indeed to sin, but alive to God in Christ Jesus our Lord."**[2] When it comes to opportunities for sin, we increasingly learn to say, "I'm dead to that." We are instructed to **"Set your minds on things that are above, not on things that are on earth."**[3]

So no, we can't be uberpositive contrary to the Bible, but must again balance the picture by presenting an example of someone from the Old Testament who failed to exhibit what it means to act like a man. The man is Solomon. While he exhibited great urgency, he totally lacked the clarity that channels urgency protectively.

WHAT DOES MATTER?

Solomon's extended exploration of life is a powerful example of energy and urgency without clarity. As king, he seized the day but then had to report in Ecclesiastes the effects of everything he achieved or experienced slipping through his fingers: **"Vanity of vanities, says the Preacher, vanity of vanities! All is vanity."**[4]

Solomon confirmed three things we all know down deep. First, we work for nothing. That's what work adds up to at the end of the day. The wisest man who ever lived looked at it all, experienced it all, and had it all. And he concluded life was "vanity" or "futility." He asked, **"What does man gain by all the toil at which he toils under the sun?"**[5] "Toil" there means self-exhausting, hot sweat-producing, energy-depleting work. **"Under the sun"** refers to the sphere of observation; anywhere on earth; our shared universal experience. We all leave like we arrived—with nothing.

Second, we alter nothing. **"A generation goes, and a generation comes, but the earth remains forever."**[6] It was not much different for your great-grandparents, and it won't be much different for your great-grandchildren. Countless superficial changes don't change the central matters of life.

Third, we're satisfied by nothing. The human mind cannot create experiences that satisfy the human spirit. There's nothing in this world that your eyes can gaze upon, your body can participate in, or your stomach can feed upon that can truly satisfy you. Solomon noted, **"All things are full of weariness; a man cannot utter it; the eye is not satisfied with seeing, nor the ear filled with hearing."**[7] At the end of the day, everything in ordinary life exhausts and disappoints. Marriage is not everything I dreamed it could be or would be because it's possessed by sinful, imperfect people. Raising and growing children is filled with joys and disappointments. Ordinary life can't deliver what we ask of it—it wasn't meant to.

But extraordinary life is possible—find it. There's a better, higher, eternal life that can begin during this earthly life. It is an awesome life found in Christ! And we can live it now!

Psalm 27:4 (NKJV) says, **"One thing I have desired . . . that will I [earnestly] seek: that I may dwell in the [presence] house of the LORD all the days of my life, to behold the beauty of the LORD."** Isn't it awesome that God's Word says ordinary life can be beautiful?[8] However, there's just one thing—not ten things, not fifteen things—that brings meaning to everything else. Don't set your life up. Don't think, "When I get my family, or my house, or my finances, then I'll have everything set up for me and life will rock!" It will not! It doesn't. The harder you try to set up satisfaction for yourself apart from God, the less you'll have it. Only a central focus on Jesus Christ and all He said and did (and dwelling in His presence) can be the one thing that puts everything else in order. Even when it seems like it's falling apart.

MY CRISIS

It's easy to see the lack of clarity in another man but can you see it in yourself? Anyone reading Ecclesiastes can figure out the futility of Solomon's vain pursuit before he even gets to the final declaration, but are we as astute in analyzing our own futility? I know I wasn't. Until . . .

CLARITY IN A CRISIS

It's the phone call we all imagine but hope we never get. My PSA (prostate specific antigen), a blood test marker that, if elevated, can indicate prostate cancer, had been rising for several years and now warranted a so-called routine biopsy. I already had a pretty negative view of prostate health given the discomfort of the doctor's innocuously titled but very invasive DRE (digital rectal exam). I managed a joke, as I leaned on my elbows, my back to my doctor and gulped, "Would you mind taking your Rolex off?"

Though he felt nothing out of order, the rising PSA was a concern, so I scheduled the biopsy—an unforgettable experience that made the DRE seem like taking my temperature. A week or so later, in October 2008, I was on the way home from preaching out of town. As I sat in the back of the taxi, I turned on my phone and heard the doctor's ominous voice mail. "I have your biopsy test results and I need you to call me."

I called immediately. I remember the exact location on the freeway where I heard his verdict: "You have prostate cancer." What I was sure he would not say he did say and it changed everything for me. Though prostate cancer is curable and mine had been caught early, my scores showed a concerning velocity of increase. I was certainly no longer confident that I was on the right side of the statistics. Telling my wife and kids was very, very tough. They were shocked and tearful as we held hands and prayed. Informing the church, our fellowship of churches, and our broadcast family I had cancer was the last thing I wanted to do, but I needed their prayers too. After careful research I chose ten weeks of proton radiation therapy at Loma Linda University Medical Center in Southern California.

The time from the end of diagnosis late in 2008 to my first test indicating successful treatment in June 2009 altered my clarity forever. Facing your mortality and a possible premature exit from this life brings into focus the things that matter most. I took a ton of time to journal and reflect during those eight months. I wanted to **"stand firm in the faith,"** and I was getting a lot of clarity on what that meant. It wasn't like I needed to heal my marriage, come back to God, or break an addiction. If you need to do any of those things, I pray that a crisis will give you the focused clarity needed to accomplish those important goals. I had been a pastor for twenty-five years at the time and through this crisis was blessed with significant insight into patterns of relating to others and leading our church that had to change. See the next study for some of those lessons.

QUESTIONS FOR REFLECTION

1. Do you agree with Solomon's assessment that life, though beautiful, is ultimately futile without an eternal purpose? Why or why not?

2. To what degree do you find yourself aiming at certain temporal things you hope will bring life special meaning? How is that going?

3. In what ways is Jesus Christ at the center of all you do? How does He bring clarity to your priorities?

Prayer:

Lord,
Thank You for making the world such a beautiful, challenging, even dangerous place. But thank You for also warning me that I was designed to live in this world in fellowship with You. Teach me to enjoy this life fully as a gift and temporary experience without ever expecting it to meet my hunger for eternity and for You. Teach me what it means to make You and Your glory the first priority in every aspect of my life. In Jesus' name I pray, amen.

NEXT TIME:
LET ME INTRODUCE YOU TO A MAN OF CLARITY

20

PAUL'S CLARITY

Brothers, I do not consider that I have made it my own. But one thing I do: forgetting what lies behind and straining forward to what lies ahead, I press on toward the goal for the prize of the upward call of God in Christ Jesus.[1]

THE APOSTLE PAUL suffered a great deal during his years of preaching the gospel and planting churches. His hardships came in many forms:

- Alexander and Hymenaeus[2] are just two of the many who claimed to be Christians but fought against Paul's ministry.
- After preaching in Lystra, Paul was stoned and dragged out of the city as if dead.[3]
- Paul was beaten, at times severely.[4]
- He was imprisoned multiple times.[5]
- Paul suffered shipwreck and almost drowned.[6]
- He was forsaken by close friends like Demas.[7]

Given his suffering, it is no surprise that Paul expresses some of the greatest clarity God has given to the church. Here are just a few from memory:

- To live is Christ; to die is gain.
- Work out your salvation with fear and trembling.
- I am crucified with Christ.
- I endure all things for the sake of the elect.
- Set your affection on things above.
- Nothing can separate us from the love of God.
- I have fought the good fight, I have finished the race, I have kept the faith.

Notice the very last one, **"kept the faith."**[8] What does Paul mean by those words written in the back of his last epistle, from a Roman prison, shortly before his execution? In previous studies we've looked at the faith as referring to God's Word as well as the gospel of Jesus Christ. **"Kept the faith"** is the final report from a lifetime of standing firm in the faith. Keeping the faith isn't a two-minute drill; it's long obedience and faithfulness over years. When Paul declared he kept the faith, he meant first of all, "I have kept it personally." Both of his letters to Timothy begin with Paul's personal testimony of consistent trust in Christ. He wasn't urging others to do what he wasn't doing. He could tell the Corinthians, **"Be imitators of me, as I am of Christ."**[9] Second, Paul kept the faith by protecting it from distortion. In Galatians 1:8 he wrote, **"But even if we or an angel from heaven should preach to you a gospel contrary to the one we preached to you, let him be accursed."** Third, he kept the faith by passing it on to others. Faith doesn't grow or deepen when we cower in secrecy. Faith strengthens as we go public. For Paul, standing firm in the faith meant keeping it personally, keeping it pure, and keeping it going. Through his suffering, God gave him immense clarity about what keeping the faith is all about.

MY CLARITY

Paul's clarity and resulting ministry impact were massively enhanced through the suffering God allowed him to endure. In my own small way, I can testify to the same. My season of trials mentioned in the last study involved far more than just my cancer. Included were a prodigal child, a dying mother, and a financial crisis in our church that was overshadowed by a power struggle in our leadership. After undergoing daily radiation at the hospital in Loma Linda, California, I had my afternoons free to walk, think, pray, and journal. God revealed to me a deep pattern of what I thought was peacekeeping but was actually people pleasing.

I had preached against it, counseled others to overcome it, but deep inside I had to confess that a lot of the struggle I experienced in ministry was because of expectations that had grown in good people through my conflict avoidance. I love people and love to care for them but found it very difficult to engage with anyone in a way that threatened their glad-hearted involvement in the ministry. This was less and less true with the typical congregant but actually worsened over time with significant leaders. I alternated between extended seasons of enablement and brief seasons of angry confrontation over matters I had postponed for a time due to a persistent problem with the fear of man. A proverb begins, **"The fear of man lays a snare,"**[10] and I have certainly seen that to be true.

The pressure on pastors to cater to people's expectations is immense, and over the years I struggled to recover from the first confrontation I endured as a pastor. We started Harvest Bible Chapel with a group of eighteen people, some of whom are still with us today. However, eighteen months in we had grown to about four hundred people, and the main leader of the group that hired me became increasingly frustrated with the church not going as he had planned. Looking back, my fear of conflict and rejection played heavily into the specific circumstances and only heightened his own issues. The result was 150 of our 400-member congregation leaving, nearly causing the church to collapse. People I loved dearly were caught up in the conflict and we were devastated personally.

I wish I could have seen then that I was also damaged. In time I was able to forgive and let go of the particular injustices I felt, even being reconciled to the main protagonist shortly before his passing into the Lord's presence. What lingered was a low-level, nagging fear that it would happen again, and it did. Boundaries with others were not properly maintained, conflict was avoided, expectations of influence and privilege were allowed to grow all in an effort to avoid another blowout. If that sounds innocent,

I can assure you it is not, because eventually, inevitably, it always came out in a way far more damaging than if I had simply dealt with conflict in a healthy and more immediate way.

STILL WORKING ON IT

In 2000 my book *I Really Want to Change, So Help Me God* came out with Moody Publishers. The book grew out of my study of Romans 6–8 and my desperate search for a way to get victory over my besetting sin of outbursts of anger. I was generally very happy, upbeat, and encouraging to others, but if I felt taken advantage of by people I had tried to "kill with kindness," I would inevitably reach a boiling point and handle the problem badly. I didn't swear or throw things, and over time seldom even raised my voice, but I would put someone in their place with a force that led them to change the subject from the wrong they were doing to the way I handled it. Worse, I didn't know when it was coming. I would love and give and pray and wait and plead and beg for change, but at some uncertain point I would abandon that plan in a moment of frustration sometimes injuring the person I had tried so hard to help.

When I began to address this issue in my life aggressively almost fifteen years ago, I thought eventually it would simply go away, that I would reach a place where it never happened again. Sadly, that hasn't happened yet. The growth I have seen has been in three areas: first, the length of time between failures has become much longer; second, the amount of time it takes to see my fault and apologize has become much shorter; and third, my awareness of where I might be tempted so I can avoid the situation altogether has become acute. Less failure, less severe, fewer excuses, but still not perfect.

SUFFERING MADE THE DIFFERENCE

Suffering related to circumstances beyond my control, suffering related to consequences of my besetting sin, and suffering caused by others who refused to see their own sin. In all these instances, the Lord has been at work, refining my focus upon personal holiness, amplifying my ministry through very humbling experiences, and reminding me repeatedly to extend grace not just to the gracious but to those who lack a grace I took too long to come to myself.

QUESTIONS FOR REFLECTION

1. What crisis has God allowed in your life at this time?

2. What issues is He giving you clarity about that you have struggled to see?

3. What action would God want you to take based on the clarity He is giving?

4. How does that action reflect a **"standing firm in the faith"**?

5. Will you commit to talking to a brother in Christ today about your clarity and intended action, asking him to pray and support your decision?

Prayer:

Thank You, Father, for Your sovereignty in all things. Your Word is true when it asserts that no trial is joyful for the moment. *Thank You, though, that* "later it yields the peaceful fruit of righteousness to those who have been trained by it." *I praise You for using this crisis in my life to bring me clarity on a needed action. Please grant me the needed courage to follow through on this clarity today. In advance and by faith, I praise You for what You are doing in my life. In Jesus' great name, amen.*

NEXT TIME:
MAKING SURE THE **WHY** WE DO
AND **WHAT** WE DO ARE IN HARMONY

21

CLARITY IN CONFLICT

*And Samuel said, "Has the Lord as great delight
in burnt offerings and sacrifices, as in obeying the
voice of the Lord? Behold, to obey is better than
sacrifice, and to listen than the fat of rams."*[1]

A FEW YEARS AGO WE WERE COMING back from Scotland with
my oldest son and about fifteen men in our church. Back then, planes had
large movie screens in the cabins. The featured film on that flight was a
horrific burlesque (it's the only word I could use to describe it) of extremely scantily clad women that we were forced to see life-size right in
front of us all. My son was just a senior in high school at the time. And I
sat there as father and trip leader feeling urgency rise as clarity declined.

I don't remember what happened next or after that as it was just a blur.
The next thing I clearly remember was standing in the plane's bathroom
with the cassette of the movie in my pocket. I had removed the offending
tape from the unattended player in the galley. I was thinking, *Now what*!?!

I couldn't stay in the bathroom forever, and I could hear people outside the door, inquiring, "What happened? Where's the MOVIE?!? This
isn't funny!" Eventually, I tried to sneak out of the bathroom and into

my seat, but my actions hadn't gone unnoticed. I heard people around me muttering, "That's HIM right there!?! He has the MOVIE. That's the GUY!?!" Before long, the chief flight attendant approached me and asked, "Sir, did you take the movie?"

I didn't answer him.

Exasperated, he said, "Either you answer me or I am going to bring the pilot back here."

I said, "Oh great. Go get him. Tell him everything is out-of-control back here and that you can't handle it. He will *love* that." I admit to being nervous, though.

Unsure what to do next, he leaned over and said quietly, "All right. Please come with me right now!" He led me back to the galley and confronted me between the coffeemaker and the food carts. "Sir, do you have the tape?"

"It's in my pocket," I admitted.

He seemed genuinely puzzled as he asked, "Why did you take the movie?"

I tried my best to be firm and gracious in my response. "Because you have no business showing that filth. And you shouldn't be forcing it on people. I am a pastor and I have fifteen men from my church with me. I strongly object to being subjected to this film on the plane."

Interestingly, the flight attendant paused and said, "I couldn't agree with you more. I am ashamed we were showing that movie. If you give it to me, I won't put it back on."

"PHEW!" I said as I handed over the tape.

In the aftermath of that experience, I felt proud about the urgency expressed in that action, but over the years I have reflected upon how much worse that could have ended and what happens when urgency trumps clarity. I was right but wrong in the way I was right; therefore, wrong.

This is where the lie of the Enemy comes in. John 8:44 says Satan is a liar and the father of lies. He captures and conquers men's lives through his convincing lies, often nullifying good intentions with wrongful actions that seemed manly in the moment but in the end lacked the balancing power of clarity. Adam believed the lie he could be equal with God and down he went. Judas believed the lie that Jesus was leading the mission off course and chose to betray Him. Men who love the Lord, doing right things but doing them in the wrong way, in the wrong amount, and at the wrong time demonstrate the devious nature of our enemy.

Why is this issue so common? Fathers take an important stand with an adolescent child in rebellion, but do it in a way that makes the problem worse. Husbands take leadership in their homes but not through selfless loving service. Instead, they abuse their authority for selfish ends. The lie of Satan is, "As long as you're doing right things, your method doesn't matter." This single issue is pulling down Christian men everywhere.

SAUL KNEW IT BUT HE DIDN'T DO IT

Saul was the first king of Israel, chosen by God and anointed by Samuel. At first he seemed like a good pick. The new king looked noble and acted humble. He wasn't sure he wanted to be king—a positive sign. But no sooner did the crown settle on his head than Saul began to make serious mistakes.[2] Like a drowning man, Saul went down three times and didn't come up. First, he disobeyed. He dabbled in disobedience when he offered sacrifices himself[3] and issued a rash vow,[4] then plunged into defiance by ignoring God's direct instruction in the matter of Agag and the Amalekite plunder.[5]

Saul went down a second time when he tried to excuse his actions. There is no defense for disobedience. Saul tried four different types of excuse to avoid admitting his sin: he claimed justified disobedience ("I disobeyed but had a good reason"); he claimed partial obedience ("I obeyed partially"); he blamed others for the disobedience ("My fear of others made me disobey"); and he blamed others for causing him to disobey ("They made me do it"). Many things make our sinful choices understandable while nothing makes them excusable.

Sadly, the king went down for the third time when he claimed his accumulated excuses should be enough to restore his standing with God when he refused to repent of his disobedience. Throughout their interaction, Samuel hammered the truth we need to hear: **"Has the Lord as great delight in burnt offerings and sacrifices, as in obeying the voice of the Lord? Behold, to obey is better than sacrifice, and to listen than the fat of rams."**[6]

This is the critical point in the story. The Bible says that **"we all fall in many ways."** None of us can say, "I never failed the Lord." And because none of us can attain perfection, we must at times be confronted about our sin. God uses His Word, a friend, or a personal circumstance to make His point. All of a sudden our failure is brought up in front of us like a mirror: "This is what you look like."

What we do when we're exposed to our sin is one of the most crucial moments in our lives. Typically we resort to one of Saul's excuses: we falsely claim obedience or partial obedience, blame others outright, or blame them for pressuring us. But no excuse outweighs disobedience. No alternative is equivalent to obedience, including sacrifices or doing right things but doing them in the wrong way, in the wrong amount, and at the wrong time.

Some decisions can't be undone. You could destroy your life by 5:00 tonight. And would God forgive you? Yes, He would forgive you. But would you bear the consequences of that decision for the rest of your life? Yes, you would! Don't ever confuse God's forgiveness and consequences. Galatians 6:7 (NKJV) says, **"Do not be deceived: God is not mocked, for whatever a man sows, that he will also reap."** You harvest what you plant. A repentant Saul would have been forgiven, but his family had lost the throne, and nothing would change that. We make choices and we live with them for the rest of our lives.

We must be very clear about sin and what to do when we realize we've sinned. A close friend of mine told me a story I have seen echoed in so many others:

My little six-year-old boy was dragging one morning, so I asked why he was so tired. He said, "I couldn't sleep."

I said, "What kept you up?"

He looked at me for a moment and then started to cry. Through his sobs he said, "I lied to my teacher yesterday. She asked me if I was talking and I said I wasn't but I was."

I said, "Well, that was a lie, wasn't it?"

And he said, "Yeah."

I put my hand on his shoulder and said, "Come on, let's ask the Lord for forgiveness." I listened to my son pray, "Lord, please forgive me." Then I took him to school and he told the teacher, "I'm sorry I lied," and reminded her of the circumstances.

And she said, "Oh, did you? Well I can tell you learned a good lesson. Thank you for telling me." And she pulled him in close. His face was just beaming afterward.

Jesus said, **"Unless you turn and become like children, you will never enter the kingdom of heaven."**[7] Unlike Saul, when we see our sin we have to be tender and broken about it. And like a little child, we have to come to the Lord. God is waiting for your repentance, and when you give it, He runs to love and gladly forgives you.

QUESTIONS FOR REFLECTION

1. What examples from your life illustrate the point that what's right can be done in ways that are wrong?

2. Which of Saul's four tactics of excuse create the biggest problem for you? What are you going to do about it?

3. As a result of mistakes, what have you learned about the difference between gut reactions and wise responses?

4. How do you practice repentance (see 1 John 1:9)?

5. How do you keep God's forgiveness separate from consequences?

Prayer:

Father God,
Forgive me for thinking I can avoid the truth about myself
with excuses. Teach me to be ruthless in rejecting self-
righteousness and self-justifications. Increase my sensitivity
about excusing instead of confessing and repenting. Keep me
from trying to substitute cheap sacrifice for costly obedience.
I realize that complete obedience is not in me, but that You
are willing to increase my obedience to a far greater level than
I can ever hope to on my own. Thank You for Your promise of
participation, "for it is God who works in you, both to will and to
work for his good pleasure."[8] *In Jesus' name, amen.*

NEXT TIME:
THINKING ABOUT THE CLARITY OF GOD

22

CLARITY— THE FATHER PERSONIFIES IT

In the year that King Uzziah died I saw the Lord sitting upon a throne, high and lifted up; and the train of his robe filled the temple.[1]

TO ME, THE MOST COMPELLING DESCRIPTIONS in Scripture are the throne-room scenes. I love the overwhelming and consuming finality of the great white throne in Revelation 20, where before God's presence **"earth and sky fled away," "the dead, great and small, [stood] before the throne,"** and **"if anyone's name was not found written in the book of life, he was thrown into the lake of fire."**[2] I'm drawn to the awesome, unquestioned authority pictured. He is God. We are not. All the mishmash of opinion and relativity will fall fast before the throne of God's final judgment. I love the clarity of it.

Another cherished throne-room scene opens the prophetic book of Ezekiel. Here the prophet uses the words *likeness* or *appearance* thirty times as he stumbles and strains to describe something unlike anything he has ever seen before. His mind is blown, his adjectives don't work, and he is completely overcome as he concludes, **"Such was the appearance of the likeness of the glory of the Lord. And when I saw it, I fell on my face."**[3] God is ineffable (indescribable) glory and He **"dwells in unapproachable light."**[4] The Lord told Moses, **"No man can see Me and live!"**[5] I truly love the way the Scriptures set right our understanding about God's perfections with piercing clarity.

However, my all-time favorite throne-room scene is found in Isaiah 6. God allowed Isaiah a glimpse of His holiness like no human being had ever seen. The familiar phrase **"In the year that King Uzziah died I saw the Lord sitting upon a throne"** introduces a scene that not only gripped the prophet but still blows away the idea of a comfortable, manageable God we've fashioned for ourselves. God (John 12:41 makes it clear Isaiah was seeing the preincarnate Christ in all His glory) sits in stunning, sovereign, absolute control over His domain. His throne is **"high and lifted up,"**[6] the train of His robe fills the temple, and the space reverberates with magnificent angels calling, **"Holy, holy, holy is the Lord of hosts; the whole earth is full of his glory!"**[7] Holiness means a lot of things: different, set apart, not like us, pure. In holiness, nothing is blurry or undefined. Nothing is relative or in transition. Holiness means everything is perfect, settled, and going to stay that way.

Now that is a view of God we have lost in the church. Preferring the comforting messages of certain attributes of God, our lives have become a trifling with His holiness. We desperately need to regain this view of the highness and the holiness of God. His holiness is the ultimate clarity.

It is absolutely astounding that God calls each of us to **"be holy, for I am holy."**[8] The clarity that our heavenly Father expresses in perfection is the holiness that He wants to express through us. Because His ways are perfect and His plans are settled; because His Word is perfect and His judgments are just, He desires each of us as men to be moving in the direction of holiness.

Yet how often as men:

- we waver when our holy God calls us to remain **"steadfast"** and **"immovable."**[9]
- we fail to lead in such a way that **"for me and my house, we will serve the LORD."**[10]
- we **"go limping between two opinions"** when **"if the LORD is God, follow Him."**[11]
- we wander or fall when He tells us to **"stand firm in the faith."**[12]
- we stumble along instead of walking **"in a manner worthy of the calling to which you have been called."**[13]

EVERY SECOND MATTERS

Call it a midlife crisis if you want to, but when I turned fifty I bought a Harley Davidson motorcycle. I had wanted one all my life but feared that my fascination with going fast could end with finality and never took the risk of owning one. By the time I was closing in on thirty years married and an "empty nest," though, I figured I had mellowed enough to negate the risks, so I jumped in. I also like the "Harley style." Leather, chrome, beards, wife on back, regular folk who tell it like it is. Perfect? Actually, a few hundred men in our church ride Harleys, so I had tons of guys to ride with and we started a little outreach called "Harvest Rides."

At first I was nervous. I had ridden my friend's Honda 250 as a student, but that was a long time ago and this motorcycle was three or four times heavier. I practiced on a smaller bike at first and passed my special permit test at the Illinois Department of Transportation with flying colors. I practiced for six months with immense caution until I could stop on a dime, swerve to miss a sudden something in the road, and anticipate the crazy actions of other motorists almost, it seemed, before they even occurred.

As I got into my second and third, then my fourth summer in the saddle, I noticed that I was becoming a very confident rider. I wasn't the least bit nervous anymore. My range increased on special trips with the church guys— over to the camp in Michigan, and up to the Harley factory in Milwaukee, Wisconsin. I was a Harley rider and loving every minute of it. As my confidence grew so did my ability to relax and enjoy the wind and sun, until . . .

I was riding to meet Kathy for a train ride to downtown Chicago for a long walk and some lunch. It was sunny and clear and as I casually followed the mini yellow school bus, I had decided not to even pass. "I'm not in a hurry, why risk it? Just enjoy the scenery." Then SKID< SLAM<CRASH!

I had been looking, just for a second, to the side at a beautiful forest preserve, but on a motorcycle you can never lose your focus. I did. What I hadn't remembered to remember was that school buses stop at all railway crossings. When my eyes came back to the road, the bus was standing still and I was closing on it at forty miles per hour. I slammed on the brakes, front and back, but in an instant I realized I was too close and about to pound the bus hard. I quickly veered right, attempting to clear the corner and ride out my stop on the shoulder but . . . I didn't make it. My left front handle grip caught the right rear corner of the bus; my front tire fender crumpled at impact, not quite fitting under the bus. My left roll bar slammed the bus corner, bending around and forcing my foot into the engine. The impact nearly halted the bike, throwing it out away from me to the right. Somehow I was enabled to plant my left foot without slipping, and the bike slid out from under me into the guardrail and I stumbled forward without falling.

Later the Harley dealership told me that the bike was totaled, but I only had a small bruise behind my left big toe. How different that story could have been. What if I had turned left instinctively but into traffic? What if I had not looked back for another second and struck the bus without braking? What if my foot was crushed against the bike, or I went down with it? No doubt God spared my life and preserved my health, for which I praise Him.

The lingering lesson is how fast, fast, fast it all happened. As men we cannot take our eyes off the road for even a second. One bad moment can destroy a lifetime of careful watching. One weak, selfish decision can crash a decade of keeping your eyes on the road. God grant to us Holy Throne-Room clarity at all times in every situation so that what we are really living for doesn't crash before our eyes.

QUESTIONS FOR REFLECTION

1. In what area of your life today might you be going forward without the clarity you need to be sure of the desired outcome?

2. What have been the consequences you have experienced for living with a foggy uncertainty?

3. What makes it hardest for you to press for clarity where it is lacking?

4. How can you **"stand firm in the faith"** so that urgency does not rule over clarity?

5. Is there someone at home, work, or church you need to call today to arrange a conversation to gain greater clarity?

Prayer:

Dear Father in heaven,
You are holy, holy, holy. The earth is full of Your glorious presence and Your holiness is infinite. Thank You that clarity in thought and deed is perfected in Your holy nature. My mind is blown as I contemplate Your call for me to holy clarity in all of my actions. I praise You for placing this restriction on my passion as a man. From the depth of my heart, I ask that my urgent watching would be perfected by Your holy clarity so that I will not simply act as You call men to act, but will do it in a way that causes benefit and not harm. I pray for the courage to act today on behalf of those who trust me in every sphere of my life. Let my passion be protected with a holy clarity that reflects Your perfect nature. In Jesus' name, amen.

NEXT TIME:
JESUS AND HIS AWESOME CLARITY

23

THE CLARITY
OF CHRIST

*For I have come down from heaven, not to do
my own will but the will of him who sent me.*[1]

GREATEST MOVIE OF ALL TIME (I will not argue this point): *Braveheart*! No research needed to write this. William Wallace from Sterling rallies the men of Scotland to throw off the shackles of English enslavement and live as freemen. Wallace's courage in opposing injustice and standing against the corrupt Scottish leaders ensnared in self-interest at the expense of their own people is truly inspirational. He stands alone for a righteous cause, rallies others to sacrificially join him, and spends himself to the end for a worthy mission that costs him everything.

The battle scenes are epic. The climactic vicious betrayal and murder of Wallace, who refuses to recant his life mission of Scottish freedom, is very moving. As he is stretched out on a rack and grimly tortured, the jeering crowd listens in to hear if he will renounce his cause and fellow freedom fighters. Instead, he throws his head back in defiance and cries out, "FREEEEEEEDOOOOOOM!"

Sends shivers down my back just typing those words. What is more awesome than seeing a man engage his God-given strength in a mission that matters and benefits those unable to fight for themselves? When a quality man is acting with urgency *and* clarity, God is going to do some awesome things. Sadly though, we are often urgent about the wrong things and unclear about what matters.

JESUS KNOWS WHAT MATTERS

Jesus Christ is the personification of quality manhood and the impact made when urgency is tempered by clarity. At the church I pastor, I have just completed a series on the gospel of John, and I'm at a new high watermark in my familiarity with the life of Christ. Jesus Christ was all about clarity.

- Christ was clear about timing—He frequently stated **"My hour has not yet come, the hour is near, and the hour has come."**[2] For three years He kept close watch on the clock so that His hour of suffering arrived at the precise moment, not a minute too soon or too late.
- Christ was clear about conflict—Though frequent attempts were made to goad Him into inflammatory conversations, Christ studiously avoided silly disputes and profitless wrangling.[3]
- Christ was clear about compassion—I have always been touched by the scenes where Jesus overrides the disciples' controls and welcomes the little children, when He looked over the crowds and wept for them as **"sheep without a shepherd."**[4] I love the compassion of Christ for the multitudes and His tender care for the sick and poor.
- Christ was clear about mission—Even when He was young and His family questioned His interest in the temple, He replied, **"Did you not know that I must be in my Father's house?"**[5] He frequently stated that He came to call sinners to repentance and to give abundant life and to set people free.[6]
- Christ was clear about family—While He loved His mother, even arranging for her care from the cross, He also instructed that love

for God must be so much greater than all other love as to make love for family appear as hatred by comparison.[7]

- Christ was clear about commitment—In His teaching He declared, **"No one who puts his hand to the plow and looks back is fit for the kingdom of God."**[8] In His pattern of behavior He demonstrated the priority of **"seek[ing] first the kingdom of God"**[9] and showing all how to **"love the Lord your God with all your heart and with all your soul and with all your mind and with all your strength, and your neighbor as yourself."**[10]

- Christ was clear about His own identity—He stated, **"Unless you believe that I am he** [God] **you will die in your sins,"**[11] **"I and my Father are one,"**[12] and **"Whoever who has seen me has seen the Father."**[13]

The list above could be much longer. In summary, Christ knew who He was, why He came, what was worth His time, how long He had, and exactly what to do to advance His mission. I am absolutely and constantly overwhelmed by the clarity Christ exhibited to channel His urgency. Clarity with urgency leads to unparalleled productivity.

DON'T TAKE YOUR CLARITY FOR GRANTED

I have three brothers (no sisters). One is older and two younger and I thank God for each of my brothers and how God has used them in my life. Just younger than me is my brother Todd. By his own admission he was the prodigal who took a lot longer to find his way home. We both did some pretty foolish things in high school and Todd always carried the guilt. I was blessed to connect with a church that poured into my life and challenged me to lead others. Todd had a falling-out with that same church and didn't find his way back into God's house for many years. By the time I was preaching the Bible, my brother, whom I love dearly, was battling addiction and finding it hard to get over some harsh treatment he had experienced from a group of people he badly needed.

I believe my brother would want me to share his story as a warning and encouragement. In God's kindness Todd did get his life on track in every way that really matters. His wife loved the Lord; his kids were growing in the faith; but somewhere, something unresolved, patterns from the past, called out to Todd in a way that seemed to haunt him. He took my mom's awful death from ALS very hard and just didn't take care of himself the way he needed to. The way his family needed him to. When his marriage began to suffer, because he loved his wife dearly, he suffered even more himself and his health deteriorated to the point where he had a massive stroke.

A dog saved his life, waking a friend to call an ambulance as Todd lay lifeless on the floor well after midnight. Emergency surgery and highly skilled medical personnel kept him alive but couldn't reverse the damage. Todd has been in a hospital for a very long time now, and while we know God does miracles, he may not ever be able to come home. Todd is conversational, but battles a stroke aftereffect doctors call "neglect." He does not fully know that he has a left side. He shaves his face but cannot see that the left side is unshaven. He sends texts but doesn't know they are nearly illegible. He quotes the Bible, sings our favorite worship songs, showers affection on his kids, and loves the Lord. But my dear brother Todd may never again have a full capacity for clarity. I weep to write these words. Please pray for my brother Todd.

I just preached the funeral of a forty-seven-year-old friend and man in our church who died of a massive heart attack on the way to work. Also named Todd, this man was a discipler of men, and the front of our chapel was crowded with crying men coming to grips with the loss of their leader. The two young men who married Todd's two oldest daughters stood and pledged to take his place, seeming like little kids stumbling around in Daddy's "way too big" shoes. God will help them, but the hole this man left is massive.

Jesus Christ lived with immense clarity. My brother Todd can't anymore; my friend Todd can't either. Every day is precious; every day is a gift from God. Men are called to live with and bring clarity, applying ourselves to what matters and lasts. Let's live today with that kind of clarity, while we still can.

QUESTIONS FOR REFLECTION

1. What story from the life of Christ do you most admire for His demonstrated clarity in the midst of confusion?

2. Why is it essential that we achieve the clarity of acting for the sake of others and not ourselves?

3. In what situation have you acted courageously to advance God's purposes, and what was the outcome?

4. In what situation have you lacked the needed clarity and applied urgency in a way that made things worse?

5. Who in your life is most in need of your courage as a man, and would you be willing to talk to him today and offer yourself to help in any way that is needed?

Prayer:

Father God,
Thank You for Your selfless giving love that acted on my behalf to provide Christ as my Savior. Please help me to see the ways that I can more closely follow His example of clarity. Please increase my hunger for Your Word and specifically for deeper reflection on the example of Christ in the Gospels. I ask today for the clarity I need to apply myself to specific situations You want to affect. I ask You to use me in a way that builds up and brings constructive change. Protect me from actions that would hinder what You are trying to accomplish. Grant to me eyes to see with clarity and courage to act with urgency. In Jesus' name, amen.

NEXT TIME:
WHAT WARNING SYSTEM DO YOU HAVE IN PLACE?

24

THIS IS NOT A TEST

But I say, walk by the Spirit, and you will not gratify the desires of the flesh.[1]

THE COLD WAR WAS A PERIOD OF INTENSE global confrontation backed up by a nuclear threat everyone knew could make most of the world uninhabitable for the few who might survive the unleashing of those weapons. Beginning shortly after World War II and lasting until the collapse of the Soviet Union in 1991, the Cold War was an ominous, fear-inducing time in our nation's history. The conflict was primarily called "cold" because the two main opponents never attacked each other directly. But the global "stare-down" created constant tension in the air.

I couldn't grasp this reality as a kid, but I remember the day we stood around during recess in Ontario, Canada, and watched the workmen erecting a tower two hundred feet in the air. We never climbed the tower because the first steps were too high off the ground to reach (by design, no doubt). In time the military gray blended with the scenery behind the baseball diamond and we seldom thought of the speaker in the sky. Except on Tuesday mornings at ten. With the sudden blare of the blitzkrieg siren, the teachers stopped talking and we students shook in our seats as the air raid warning system went through its regularly scheduled test. Always present, and ever ready to warn us to take cover if the Cold War heated up.

YOUR WARNING SYSTEM

Air raid sirens were erected to warn us about a nuclear attack that never came. Did you know that God has placed a warning system inside you to warn you about an attack that never ceases to assault God's designs on your life? The Bible says that Satan is **"a roaring lion, seeking someone to devour,"**[2] and he wants to feast on your soul. He does this through two main points of temptation: (1) Satan tempts us to do things God the Holy Spirit does not want us to do; (2) Satan resists our doing the things God's Spirit is prompting us to do. When Satan is tempting us, the Holy Spirit convicts us to say no. When Satan resists us doing right things, the Holy Spirit pushes us to obey. In fact, His warnings come with power to obey if we are willing to follow His lead.

You see, we cannot live the Christian life ourselves. Paul says in Galatians 5:16, **"But I say, walk by the Spirit, and you will not gratify the desires of the flesh."** This is a breakthrough truth for any believer. God has promised to live His life through you—it's not up to you to live the Christian life. Jesus said, **"I am the vine; you are the branches."**[3] All you gotta do is let the life that flows through the vine, flow into the branch— you. You don't have to *do* anything. You've just got to get out of the way and stop doing all the things that keep God from doing what He wants to do in your life. What Paul means by **"walk by the Spirit"** is essentially "live in dependence on God's Spirit."

This is a breakthrough truth because it addresses a significant problem Paul turns to: **"For the desires of the flesh are against the Spirit, and the desires of the Spirit are against the flesh** (there's a tug-of-war going on), **for these are opposed to each other, to keep you from doing the things you want to do"** (Galatians 5:17). The conflict you often feel inside is real. Verse 18 goes on, **"But if you are led by the Spirit** (if you are filled with the Spirit, if you are controlled by the Spirit), **you are not under the law."** Your flesh has a certain way of getting its needs met—it's your old nature unredeemed by Christ. It's that persistent drive to be in control of your own fate. The flesh wants to be fed, but it only feeds on sin. And it is in fierce struggle with the Holy Spirit over what's going to happen in your life. The warnings issued by the Holy Spirit are not "tests" of the system; they are broadcasts of imminent attacks.

Attentive reading of God's Word will set you up for frequent Holy Spirit warnings as He uses Scripture to set off alarms of danger in your life. As you grow spiritually, you may discover direct "prompts" God's Spirit gives, but they will always be in harmony with what God says in His Word.

The verses we looked at above, however, remind us that we are fully capable of ignoring and resisting the Holy Spirit's warnings in us. We can desire what God doesn't want us to desire. We can begin to cooperate and want what our old nature wants, desiring *against* the Holy Spirit.

We are also told we can grieve the indwelling Holy Spirit. Ephesians 4:30 says, **"And do not grieve the Holy Spirit of God, by whom you were sealed for the day of redemption."** This is the same "sealing" mentioned in Ephesians 1:13–14: **"In him you also, when you heard the word of truth, the gospel of your salvation, and believed in him, were sealed with the promised Holy Spirit, who is the guarantee of our inheritance until we acquire possession of it, to the praise of his glory."** The Holy Spirit absolutely has done the sealing that guarantees my salvation until I **"acquire possession of it."** Salvation is mine, but I won't experience all it means until heaven. Meanwhile I carry the Holy Spirit within as a deposit.

Only one time do you get baptized. Only one time do you get indwelled by the Holy Spirit. Only one time do you get sealed. But now that He's in you, don't grieve Him. The word for "grieve," *lupeo*, means "to cause pain or sorrow." J. Oswald Sanders wrote, "Grieve is a love word. One can anger an enemy, but not grieve him. The words are mutually exclusive. Only one who loves can be grieved, and the deeper the love the greater the grief."[4] The Holy Spirit, God Almighty Himself, lives within you and He loves you. And when you do things that are not pleasing to the Lord, it grieves the Holy Spirit. It means it makes Him sad.

Many things fall into the category of grieving offenses. Ephesians 4:25–29 includes numerous ways we grieve the Holy Spirit in speech and action. We all experience times when the Spirit is controlling us, and all of a sudden we get in a situation and speak out something that we shouldn't say, in our flesh. The Spirit is saddened and we are not being controlled by Him anymore. Grieving the Spirit forfeits His filling and leaves us vulnerable.

Another way we resist the Holy Spirit and His warnings involves quenching Him. First Thessalonians 5:19 says, **"Do not quench the Spirit."** The word means to *stifle* or *extinguish* God's presence. It also means to defeat His intended result and ignore His voice.

Here's the sad news, Christian. When we hinder the Holy Spirit by resisting Him, desiring against Him, grieving, quenching, and rejecting Him, we are not filled with the Spirit. And we forfeit every spiritual perk, not just the warnings. Every good thing God wants to do in my life comes through the instrumentality of the Holy Spirit: the fruit of the Spirit, understanding of God's Word, love of worship, strength in a trial, grace to forgive, compassion for the lost, comfort in heartache, boldness in witnessing, and power in ministry, all of this is *gone* when we're not filled with the Holy Spirit. Consider this a clear warning. If you are a follower of Jesus, you have a built-in early warning system that can keep you from harm and energize your obedience. Are you walking by the Spirit?

QUESTIONS FOR REFLECTION

1. How would you describe the current role of the Holy Spirit in your life?

2. When was the last time you sensed God's Spirit issuing a warning to you about a decision or action you were considering? What did you do?

3. What is holding you back from more consistent yielding to the Holy Spirit in daily living?

4. Is there, in you, a strong and growing dissatisfaction with the level of your own relationship with God? If so, use the following prayer to create a plan for the next week.

Prayer:

Heavenly Father,
I recognize I need to be filled by Your Spirit. I've trusted Christ for my salvation, so I know I have Your Spirit indwelling—but I want His filling.

I also realize that holding and guarding sin prevents filling. So I'm confessing all known sin and asking You to reveal any iniquity I'm overlooking. I will meet with some Christian friends and ask them to help me see myself better. Whatever it takes, I want to remove the hindrances that would grieve or quench Your Spirit.

Lord, I want to yield myself completely to Your purposes. Help me eliminate all secondary goals. I want to desire only what You desire for my life.

Please alert me by Your Spirit every morning to ask You to fill me. I'm counting on Your Son's promise, "If you then, who are evil, know how to give good gifts to your children, how much more will the heavenly Father give the Holy Spirit to those who ask him!" *Fill me now, Lord. I confess and ask You for these things in Jesus' name, amen.*

NEXT TIME:
WE BEGIN A NEW SECTION ENTITLED BE STRONG

BE STRONG

25

THE BATTLE TO BE STRONG

*Be watchful, stand firm
in the faith, act like men, be strong.[1]*

HAVE YOU SEEN THOSE ESPN SHOWS called *The World's Strongest Man*? It's actually amazing to watch if you can get past the occasional offensive camera angle featuring a grunting, red-faced man whose one-piece sleeveless shorts have become a thong. I love to couch-crash with my Doritos and donuts, watching men half my age lift massive stones twice my body weight like they are lifting a twig. Talk about strong! And have you seen the segment where they grab a rope and drag a tractor-trailer full of rocks down a runway? Wouldn't it be amazing to have that guy jump out from a bush next time you're stuck in the snow or mud? "Ummm, you won't need that tow truck sir, just step aside and let me lift your car out of the ditch for you." Wow!

BE STRONG

From mud wrestling to muscle cars; from driving fence posts to carrying groceries in from the garage, men love strength and are frequently called on to exhibit it. In fact, my guess is that when you read our theme verse in 1 Corinthians 16:13–14 and assessed the five imperatives of biblical masculinity, you were most comfortable with the call to strength.

The problem is that Paul's exhortation for men to **"be strong"** has little if anything to do with physical strength. In the original language of the Bible, the word translated **"be strong"** is in a perfect passive tense. This gives two important clues as to its meaning for us as men. First, because it is in the "perfect" form, the word is requiring that our strength as men be continuous action, a state of being more than a momentary muscular action. God calls us to have strength in our character and conduct, not simply a stiff upper lip in sorrow or a stubborn persistence during hardship. Secondarily, because the word is "passive voice," we know that the strength God demands He also provides. The strength does not come from a place inside us but a source beyond ourselves, namely, the Lord. This is so consistent with other biblical directives about strength and where it comes from, such as the following: **"Be strong in the Lord and in the strength of his might,"**[2] **"Be strong in the grace that is in Christ Jesus."**[3]

WHAT MEN NEED

Early in my pastoral ministry I began to travel some weekends and speak at men's retreats. I think my direct style coupled with biblical content and humor must have clicked because I got invited back to more and larger events as time went on and really enjoyed connecting with the men.

For the first several years I would begin each retreat with a survey. I would stand up and say, "I haven't decided what to preach on this weekend, at least not yet. I have come to serve you as men and want to learn what your specific areas of need are so that I can spend my energy on the issues of greatest concern in your life." That was just to get their attention, but they really freaked when I passed out blank 3 x 5 cards. "I want each of you to write down, no names please, your three greatest battles, your three greatest struggles—the issues of greatest concern and frustration to you personally." At first I did it to learn about men and their lives, but over time I did it just to let them express themselves. I didn't need to learn any more, because the answers were always the same.

Could you name the three biggest issues in a man's life in our generation? I can count them down. Number three is frustration at work, feeling stuck, unfulfilled, and unsure how to see that change. Most men don't love what they do for a living and find it really tough to live their faith in a way that is consistent with what they profess to believe at home or church.

Number two is a sense of being in over their heads at home. Among the many men who want to protect and provide for the families they love, there is a broad sense of feeling undertrained for the know-how needed, and overmatched by the challenges that come.

And . . . the number one issue facing men in our day, raised on every single honest survey card in every state and country where I took the time to ask? (Drumroll please . . .) Sexuality. No surprise there, right? Now I know sexuality is a broad category but the issues are really pretty narrow. Lust, temptation, pornography, satisfaction in marriage, attraction to others; penis problems in a thousand varieties was always the number one frustration of men reported in my survey.

JESUS ON SEX

Jesus Christ taught with clarity and urgency but without the kind of shock-jock foolishness that characterizes so much ministry in the area of sexuality today. With a little discernment you can apply many of the things Jesus said to strengthen your victory over sexual temptation. For example, when Jesus says, **"If your right eye causes you to sin, tear it out . . . And if your right hand causes you to sin, cut it off,"**[4] He may have had in mind masturbation (hand) fed by lustful images (eye). When He says, **"It is better that you lose one of your members than that your whole body be thrown into hell,"**[5] He may have had in mind the danger that a lifetime of sexual sin and disobedience evidences a person not truly born again.

Second Corinthians 5:17 says, **"If any man is in Christ he is a new creation, old things** (patterns of sexual sin) **are passing away; behold, all things** (God-honoring choices of biblical sexuality) **are becoming new."**[6] Consequently, if old patterns of sin are not passing away, the "any man" is surely not in Christ. We cannot be sure Christ was thinking of these matters specifically, but the allusion seems to be there and the application of these verses to sexual sin and victory is certainly appropriate. Unrepented, ongoing, unaltered patterns of sexual sin will take a man to hell. Yet many are living that very life, deluded by weak preaching and deceived by biblical illiteracy into thinking grace coddles the unrepentant. If your faith hasn't changed you, be sure it has not saved you. **"On that day, many will say to me, 'Lord, Lord' . . . then I will declare to them, 'I never knew you; depart from me.'"**[7]

MY JOURNEY TO SEXUAL PURITY

I was the kid with a strong sexual appetite and an early first exposure. One summer at a muddy construction site near our house, my closest friend and I found a small photo of a topless woman. We had built a fort in the cedar hedge at the rear of his backyard and carefully cleaned and dried the picture, storing it inside a juice can.

For hours we would stare at those breasts as we sat in the shade on scorching afternoons, trying to understand why this single photo had a hold on us and the monster it had awoken within us. We frequently discussed a vague feeling of guilt and the need to discard the picture but we never did. I can still bring that picture to mind. A few years later I discovered that a kind of weird uncle used to leave *Playboy* magazines stacked in the upstairs bathroom of his house. As I remember it, I frequently "had to go" when we visited his home, and I discovered in that little bathroom a world that made my mouth drop open while the oblivious adults talked downstairs for hours on end. I was probably eight or nine when this first happened, but the war had begun.

A new kind of craving called out for attention, and I remember backyard sleep-outs that necessitated a trip to the corner store. When money was lacking, one guy stuffed the porno magazines under his shirt while the other distracted the clerk. I still recall the night he caught us stealing *Hustler* and *Penthouse*, pinning us to the window on the plaza sidewalk, and pulling up our shirts to see what we were hiding. I remember being staggered by the knowing grin he gave us as he leafed through our loot and laughed, handing the mags back with pleasure and dispatching us to a long night of discovering lust. As a preadolescent I had no idea that God wanted me to **"be strong,"** let alone that He commanded me to **"flee from youthful lusts."**[8] Looking up the scriptural imperatives wouldn't have helped me anyway; I needed but didn't know the Savior who would later strengthen me.

QUESTIONS FOR REFLECTION

1. Do you agree that as men, we admire great strength in others and aspire to it ourselves? In what ways?

2. When have you most needed strength and felt most humbled by where you lacked it?

3. How do you respond to the knowledge that unbroken patterns of sin in all areas including sexuality are indicative of a man who is not truly following Christ?

4. What are your earliest memories of sexual temptation, and how did you handle them?

Prayer:

Father God,
I come to You today as Your man, bought and paid for by the sacrifice of Your Son. In my heart I deeply desire to be a slave to righteousness and not a slave to sin. I pray for greater levels of victory over the power of lust and longer seasons of joyful obedience to Your Word. Forgive me for the times I have allowed my desires to dehumanize and objectify people for selfish sinful purposes. Cleanse my heart and mind from images and memories that hinder my desire to obey Your command to

"be strong." I welcome Your strength today to conquer any lust lingering in my heart and ask that I could walk today in genuine victory and flee any temptation I encounter for Your glory. In Jesus' name, amen.

NEXT TIME:

THE PROBLEM OF A DIVIDED HOUSE

26

THE STRENGTH OF AUTHENTICITY

And if a house is divided against itself,
that house will not be able to stand.[1]

IT IS HARD TO IMAGINE NOW THAT HIS speech at the capitol in Springfield, Illinois, led not to victory but to defeat. In fact, the wording is so compelling it's considered a discourse for the ages. It was delivered long before he was numbered among the outstanding leaders of all time, and well before he was respected as the premier president in our nation's history. Many years before he was president at all, during an unsuccessful bid to be elected the singular senator from the Prairie State, Abraham Lincoln gave his "House Divided" speech on June 16, 1858.

Arguing that a nation could not long endure opposite opinions on the morality of slavery, Lincoln predicted that the nation would have to settle the argument in order to escape the crushing dissonance of living with both impossibly coexistent viewpoints.

In Lincoln's own words,

"A house divided against itself cannot stand. I believe this government cannot endure, permanently, half slave and half free. I do not expect the Union to be dissolved—I do not expect the house to fall—but I do expect it will cease to be divided. It will become all one thing or all the other. Either the opponents of slavery will arrest the further spread of it, and place it where the public mind shall rest in the belief that it is in the course of ultimate extinction; or its advocates will push it forward, till it shall become lawful in all the States, old as well as new—North as well as South."

Lincoln was right. Morality and decency conquered the prejudicial injustice and horror of slavery, but not without a fierce and extended conflict and incalculable suffering. The Civil War was the costly resolution of an untenable division.

DOES THAT SOUND FAMILIAR?

"A house divided against itself cannot stand." It seems like we have heard that somewhere before, and I don't think it was a vague recollection of Civil War week during my high school American history class. Amazingly, in a quick Google search of the speech Lincoln gave more than 150 years ago, I could not find a single attribution of those words. Do you know their source? They are the words of Christ, of course, from Mark 3:25: **"And if a house is divided against itself, that house will not be able to stand."**

Lincoln was predicting the domination or suppression of slavery because the cohabitation of such opposing viewpoints would necessarily have to end. When He spoke these words, Jesus had just cast out a demon and was accused by the Pharisees of being from Satan because the demons submitted to Him. Christ's counterargument was that Satan would never cast out Satan, which was irrefutable to say the least. He taught us that anything attacking itself would not long endure.

By reading into the fourth section of this book, you are demonstrating great desire to act like a man in everything those words mean. The danger is if you have not yet won a decisive victory and wielded your sword across the neck of unrestrained lust in your life, your house is headed for a fall. And with immense sadness, those who love you will lament, **"and great was the fall of it."**[2]

STRONG MEANS AUTHENTICITY

Nothing weakens a man like hypocrisy, wavering between two opinions. James 1:8 says, **"A double-minded man** [is] **unstable in all his ways."** Sadly, after thirty years in ministry I have had a front-row seat to the inevitable wreckage that always follows a divided house, a hypocritical lifestyle, and a double mind that declares, "I want to honor God AND my secret selfishness." A divided heart is like an engine trying to run with water in the gas tank. The problem is not always sexual—it could be financial, ego driven, or love of power—but sadly, most often it includes a sexual component. A good man with a wonderful family gets bored and frustrated. Before too long, he is fixated on the man who has greater freedom than he does or on the woman who seems more exciting than what is familiar. After weeks or months of thinking this way, the man has jeopardized his conviction about what matters most. As we learn from the children of Israel in the wilderness, who craved meat, they gorged on it until it ran out their nostrils.[3]

When we dwell on our desires, yielding is just a matter of time. Strength wears away in the divided heart until the dark side takes over. And men who once seemed invincible in their authentic strength fall, first in their minds, but soon after in shameful living color for all to see. When that happens, people shake their heads and shrug their shoulders. "How did this happen? He was so strong!" But the crisis of discovery is just revealing a draining of strength that has been seeping away during a thousand little compromises over a long period of time.

MY JOURNEY TO SEXUAL PURITY (PART 2)

As I entered puberty, I discovered as we all do that this sexual attraction thing is more than just a mental pleasure or solo sport. I homed in with my friends on some of the local beauties our age for a few fumbling exchanges with girls who seemed just as curious as we were, allowing minor hand tours that were more exploration than sexual encounter. However, it was another step in the wrong direction for a guy who had been wisely advised to wait for the marriage bed, which God declares to be held in

"honor" and **"undefiled."**[4] By my early teens I professed to be a follower of Christ and was baptized, but personal pursuits and fulfillment were still competing with some success for the true place of lordship in my life. Too often Jesus Christ was not my Master but a bystander I visited with at church occasionally. When I jumped in the backseat of the family car and headed home each Sunday around noon, I guess I thought the Lord stayed in the worship center, waiting for me to return the following week. Jesus certainly didn't reign over lust in my heart and I knew nothing of His strength during those years. When temptation came, I wasn't strong because I wasn't authentic. I wasn't even trying to live a consistent life. I was the house divided and I wasn't able to stand. I didn't know the power of grace, so I felt a ton of guilt and I didn't rely on the power of the Holy Spirit, so I was weak in the face of temptation. At best, my loyalties were in constant turmoil.

WHERE THE JOY IS

The joy of following Jesus is the fellowship of living in His strength and knowing His presence as a moment-by-moment reality. If someone had said those words to me when I was fifteen, I would have looked at them like they were from Mars. Sadly, many Christian men remain where I was as a high school student, living a life of shame and defeat, completely oblivious to the strength Jesus offers and how to access it. Today I would no more trade my fellowship with Jesus for a moment of lust than you would trade a family member for a piece of licorice. Back then, I began to have a sense of how I *didn't* want to live but never understood that He is the strength.

Please hear me: Jesus doesn't *give* us strength, He IS the strength. Review study 24 to grasp how Jesus by His Spirit gives us what we need to face every challenge. If you don't know what I mean and have not experienced this reality personally, start with some genuine humility in the questions and prayer below and we will add more as we look at one of the saddest men in the Bible—the strongest and weakest man who ever lived.

QUESTIONS FOR REFLECTION

1. In what area in your life would you be most embarrassed for your friends and family to have full knowledge of your thoughts and actions?

2. In what part of your life are you most like Christ and why do you believe you have victory there versus other areas?

3. Is there anyone you can be completely candid with—who knows the deepest you with all your struggles—without judgment or condemnation?

4. Describe a time when you have forfeited God's strength through divided priorities and compromise of what really matters most to you. What did you do to resolve this and did it happen again?

5. Have you been able to be completely candid in answering these questions? Do you fear someone finding what you might write and have held back for that reason?

Prayer:

Dear Father in heaven,
I know that You desire truth in my inmost being and I want to be the kind of quality man who gives You that level of authenticity. I am seeking Your strength today to live in the victory of Christ's resurrection over all of my sins. Help me to stand against temptation in Your strength today and take every sinful thought captive so that my mind remains focused on exalting Christ today. Give me courage to abolish any wandering thoughts or

established patterns of sin that hinder Your strength from being my personal experience. I choose to walk in that strength today. In the strong name of Jesus, amen.

NEXT TIME:
WHEN STRENGTH CAN BE A REAL LIMITATION

27

THE SAMSON SYNDROME

And he awoke from his sleep and said, "I will go out as at other times and shake myself free." But he did not know that the LORD had left him.[1]

NO SINGLE NAME EPITOMIZES RAW POWER like Samson. He is easily the title-bearer for the Bible's strongest man. He was also a magnet for women and a sucker for all things sensual. On his good days he accomplished unbelievable physical feats, standing for the right and routing God's enemies. On his bad days he acted like a sex addict unable to say no to his own urges and putting all that he stood for at risk.

Those who watched Samson closely wanted to know the secret of his strength.[2] It wasn't obvious. While most of us imagine—and Bible story books depict—Samson as a muscle-bound figure, it seems unlikely people would have wondered about his strength if he was as buff as the winner of this year's Mr. Universe pageant. In other words, he was a lot stronger than he looked.

By the time he is sleeping on Delilah's couch after revealing his secret for sexual favors, we know what the secret is and we know why his power left him. Samson was incomparably strong because he was unusually yielded to God and lived by a very strict vow. When he fell into sin and betrayed his vow, his strength disappeared and he didn't even know it, declaring, "**'I will go out as at other times and shake myself free.' But he did not know that the Lord had left him.**"[3] As a result, Samson could no longer serve the Lord or use his strength. Is there anyone in the Old Testament who started out so strong and ended so shamefully? Samson, so incredibly powerful and at the same time so pathetically weak. Let's take a closer look.

BORN TO GREATNESS

Judges 13 introduces Samson through his parents, who had been barren but were given a miracle child. An angel suddenly appeared and announced to Samson's parents, "You're going to have a boy and he's going to be special. He's going to belong to Me from the day that he is born." After years of infertility, Samson's parents were delighted to worship God and committed to do what He instructed.

Samson was raised as a Nazirite, a person who took a vow to belong totally to God. Today, Christians would say we're all supposed to have taken that vow! Belonging totally to God is what the lordship of Jesus Christ is all about.

But in Old Testament days, the culture specified certain behavior to indicate God's ownership. A Nazirite vow meant that a person, first, would abstain from all wine and strong drink. It is interesting to me how often the Bible reports that people like Aaron and his descendants, Hannah, and John the Baptist who belonged totally to God stayed away from alcohol. Second, Nazirites were forbidden to touch a corpse—not a person, not an animal—nothing dead. And third, they were not allowed to cut their hair for the duration of the vow, which in Samson's case was for a lifetime. These were signs to remind him of God's ownership. When he walked by a barbershop, he thought, "Nah, I belong to God." When someone would offer him a drink, he said, "No thanks, I belong to God."

Sadly—pathetically—Samson's life did *not* belong to God; it belonged to Samson. He was a sensual person. Though he grew up under

God's blessing, his attention was drawn to pleasure like a moth to a sizzling bulb.

GOD'S STRENGTH

True to His promise, God gave Samson great strength to wield. He killed a lion with his bare hands, slaughtered a thousand Philistines with the jawbone of a donkey, and removed a massive gate from the city of Gaza in order to prove they couldn't keep him locked inside. Later a series of different bindings couldn't restrain him—until he gave Delilah the key to his strength.

DISREGARD FOR AUTHORITY

Again and again the Word of God instructs that **"The fear of the LORD is the beginning of wisdom."**[4] I praise God for a father who taught me about respect for authority and a mother who taught me the fear of the Lord. Maybe it was because Samson was their only son or because of their reverence for Samson's calling, but somehow they fell into a parental pattern of never telling him no. And Samson never learned impulse control.

Even after Samson saw the Philistine girl in Timnah,[5] he could have walked away. Instead he plunged into sin when he told his parents, **"Now get her for me as my wife."**[6] They meekly suggested he reconsider, but Samson's telling response was, **"She is right in my eyes."**[7] He didn't even consider them when he consorted with a prostitute and then chose Delilah as his next love interest. Any man who refuses or ignores the warnings of those God has placed over him is tearing the warning label off the bottle of poison and placing it in the fridge. The poison came in the form of a woman named Delilah, but by then Samson had rejected all authority beyond his own urges and the end was very near.

CAN'T FEEL THE PAIN

It is a very serious thing to allow your conscience to become calloused' Those who ignore the inner prompting to turn from evil and pursue good soon suffer **"shipwreck of their faith."**[8] What follows between

Samson, Delilah, and the Philistines is a deadly cat-and-mouse game. **"So Delilah said to Samson, 'Please tell me where your great strength lies, and how you might be bound, that one could subdue you.'"**[9]

Let me say this: men who use their strength to intimidate and manipulate women are wicked! You are practicing wickedness if the abilities God intended you to use to cover and protect your family are used instead to get your sensual way. (It is also true that women who use sex to manipulate men are behaving sinfully.)

Judges 16:5–22 records three rounds of the dangerous game: "I'll give you what you want if you tell me what I want." It's all implied in the text. You don't have to be brilliant to see it. It turns into a wicked contest between sensual people, trading on each other's weaknesses. For all his physical strength, Samson was a moral and sensual weakling.

By the time Samson was drunk on the couch, with the woman plotting his downfall and signaling the barber, he had no weapons left to fight with. He wanted only his own pleasure and was blind to God's departure.

MY OWN JOURNEY TO SEXUAL PURITY (PART 3)

The one thing that kept me from plunging headlong into fornication in high school was the fear of God my family had instilled in me. It was not lack of opportunity or lack of desire but fear of being found out that provided a measure of restraint. I surely have regrets from that time period but praise the Lord for taking hold of my life at seventeen and directing my heart to serve Him when I only had liabilities to offer. By my eighteenth year I was dating the girl I would marry, and by God's grace we saved ourselves for the honeymoon with only a few "cuts and bruises" to show for our pent-up desire.

I soon discovered, however, that a frequent, fulfilling, sexual relationship in marriage was not a cure-all for the problem of lust. In the mid-1980s the Internet was still a few years off, but take-home videos offered a temptation to watch in the privacy of your home things you would never sit through in public. I was a youth pastor at the time and realized that any double standard between what I taught the students and lived in private would forfeit God's favor upon my ministry. I also knew that my appetite for nudity that had been stoked in my childhood needed radical surgery. I found myself weak in the face of temptation but prayerfully seeking a way to avoid temptation altogether.

QUESTIONS FOR REFLECTION

1. Who have you trusted with the knowledge of your own early exposure to sensuality and ensuing struggles?

2. Why do you think Satan goes to such lengths to scatter sensual crumbs in a young man's pathway that lead him in the wrong direction?

3. How much of your personal sexual history has affected your relationship with God? How do you deal with the fact that God knows it all?

Prayer:

Father,
I know that sex is a wonderful gift from You that sin and Satan try desperately to corrupt. Thank You for marriage and the special protection for healthy sexual expression that it provides. Thank You for the powerful effects of forgiveness that so often must address ways we have misused or abused our sexuality. I pray for relationships with other men where I can disclose who I really am and experience the weight of their experiences as I pray for them.

Cure me from ever thinking, Father, that the way I treat my body doesn't somehow fit into Your plans for me. Teach me to value my sexuality and every other good gift from Your hands as one of the means by which You want to bring glory to Yourself. I pray that will be true in my life, in Jesus' name, amen.

NEXT TIME:
PAUL'S SENSUAL AWARENESS AND
MY ONGOING QUEST FOR SEXUAL PURITY

28

THE THORNY WAY

*But he said to me, "My grace is sufficient for you,
for my power is made perfect in weakness."[1]*

WHEN MOST PEOPLE THINK of the apostle Paul, they envision a man with incredible strength, but that is not the case. In fact, from a physical standpoint Paul was more like a 99-pound weakling. He may have endured stoning, shipwreck, and multiple beatings, but the Bible says that his stature was unimpressive, his appearance unattractive, and his speech contemptible. It seems Paul was more like the kid who got punched out a lot at recess and was frequently pranked by his peers—for sure not strong.

"Oh, but Paul was strong in his character," you might say. Actually, that's not the way he saw it. Consider these personal confessions of weakness from the pen of Paul:

- He feared, **"lest after preaching to others I myself should be disqualified."[2]**
- **"And, apart from other things, there is the daily pressure on me of my anxiety for all the churches."[3]**
- **"I was with you in weakness and in fear and much trembling."[4]**
- **"For I fear that perhaps when I come I may find you not as I wish, and that you may find me not as you wish."[5]**

- He asked others to pray he would be bold in proclaiming the gospel.[6]

How is it possible that a man so focused on his deficiencies and weakness was the strongest servant of the church in all of history? Or maybe the focus on weakness was not prohibitive to his strength but was actually the pathway to such immense personal strength. Insight to this matter comes to us in Paul's own words in 2 Corinthians 12.

THORNS MAKE US STRONG

A thorn. That word is only used once in the New Testament, in 2 Corinthians 12:7: **"So to keep me from becoming too conceited . . . a thorn was given me in the flesh."** It means literally *a splinter; a stake; a thorn; a small piece of wood embedded in the skin that causes pain.* And really—the pain is disproportionate to its size.

The apostle Paul is famous for his thorn. So what was it? The educated and wild guesses range from physical ailments and recurring temptations to character flaws and besetting sins, but the fact is the Bible doesn't tell us what the thorn was. If God wanted us to know, He would have told us. But because we don't know, you can think it's your thing; I think it's my thing; we all think it's the thing we suffer with. I'm just like Paul—I have a thorn. And that's not bad. We can all look into God's Word and find comfort and strength like Paul found in Christ.

A thorn is an enduring source of personal pain allowed by God for our good. Thorns are real. They are lasting, tormenting, and beneath it all, satanic. Satan's goal is to harass and torment us through our thorns. His goal is to paralyze you with fear; to pummel you into painful hopelessness; to make you think all is lost and nothing will change. That's your thorn. Whatever form it takes in attacking mind, will, or emotions, torment is Satan's purpose.

But if God's goal wasn't to use the thorn for your good, He would not have allowed it. You need to be sure of that. He has promised that **"For those who love God all things work together for good."**[7] You don't have to be able to see it; it's not up to you to have to come up with a plan to figure it out. That's not on you! It is on God to figure that out. You may never be able to figure it out, but He has promised that His goal is to use it for good.

Notice the answer that Paul gets: **"But he said to me."**[8] This is the only time in all of Paul's writings that he quotes Jesus. Acts 9:5 quotes Jesus speaking to Paul, but Paul himself never quotes Jesus speaking, except here, and about this thorn. He must have been hanging on to these words. *I have this. Jesus said it. It's done.*

"But he said to me, 'My grace is sufficient.'"[9] If you're going to get through with your thorn, you've got to have the grace. Your thorn will *crush* you without God's grace. Without grace, you will become bitter in a flash. Do you understand that God does not dispense strength and encouragement like a druggist fills a prescription? He's not like, *Here. Take two of these and call Me in the morning.* He *is* the grace. He *is* the strength. It's intimacy with Him! His presence is power! No matter what we need, Jesus is the answer when He literally says, "Sufficient for you is the grace of Me."

"But he said to me, 'Sufficient for you is the grace of me, for my strength is [completed] **in weakness.'"**[10] You never really get the grace unless you see the need for it. And even *that realization* is a grace. The grace of Jesus is not fully seen until weakness is fully experienced.

"For the sake of Christ, then, I am content with weaknesses."[11] Now, that does not mean I like the thorn, or that I want it, or that I enjoy it. Don't accept that kind of pressure from people who twist platitudes from Scripture. But I accept it. I submit to it. And I embrace it. By God's grace, I rest in it. I'm not putting my life on hold. I'm not counting the seconds until the thorn is removed. I'm not getting by and refusing to enjoy anything else. God help me. I'm living my life with the thorn. I'm relying on Christ's strength as I admit my weaknesses. The choice may not be easy, but the alternatives are all *much* harder in the long run!

This is a total paradigm shift. Strength is found in admission of weakness. God allows us to feel our weakness so we will run to Him for His strength. Only His strength is true strength. When we humble ourselves and admit our need for His strength, we are living authentically. When we live apart from God's strength and try to appear as though we are capable and confident in our own abilities, we fail miserably and repeatedly. It's hard for a man to admit he is weak. It's hard for me to write honestly about my own journey to sexual purity, but I am praying that my honesty and confession of weakness will give you permission to do the same. I am not sharing every detail like I have with a trusted friend nor should you open up to the world. However, each of us needs a couple of guys who know our secret struggles whatever they may be and can help us move out of our weakness and into God's strength. We will talk about those kind of relationships in the final section of this book.

MY JOURNEY TO SEXUAL PURITY (PART 4)

By the time we moved to Chicago in 1986, I had been married for three years and we had our first child, a son. My marriage was very fulfilling, but I was still tempted and struggled if something "to see" was available. I began to realize that completely closing the doors I had opened as a child was going to require more than a happy marriage. When the televangelist failures of 1987 hit the airwaves I was devastated. Working as a pastor during seminary in Chicago, I just couldn't see how a man would flush a ministry he spent a lifetime building for a momentary pleasure. I was filled with immense fear that the same would happen to me.

Our ministry was to young adults, including a lot of pretty young women, but I established strong boundaries, never meeting or riding alone with a woman other than my wife. Those boundaries served me well and would become the foundation for the moral fences I will tell you about up ahead. I managed those years with no serious temptation to infidelity but always lurking was the temptation to pornography, which I sometimes felt quite strongly. But through a very full schedule and a lack of availability, it was only occasionally a problem. Constant vigilance was needed to turn the channel when something provocative appeared and look away when the same happened in public. I talked with my wife at length during these years about my desire to "only have eyes for her." I am thankful for her grace and patience as I began, with her help, to tame the lion of lust. However, the battle was not over and soon the lion would roar again.

QUESTIONS FOR REFLECTION

1. What is the area of greatest weakness in your life?

2. When did you last confess this weakness to the Lord, seeking His strength?

3. Is it difficult for you to admit your struggles to yourself and others? Why?

Prayer (find a quiet place to kneel down if possible):

God,
I come before You in the name of Your strong Son, Jesus Christ. I am kneeling here because I want the posture of my body to reflect the humility in my heart. I confess to You that I am a weak man. My intentions are not stronger than my lust; my will to do right is often not stronger than the temptation around me. I confess my weakness and ask forgiveness for the times my body has not been used as an instrument of righteousness for Your glory. I desire truth in my innermost being and ask that Your grace cleanse my heart and Your strength give me victory, for apart from You I can do nothing. In Jesus' name, amen.

NEXT TIME:
A STUDY OF DAVID AND HIS STRUGGLE FOR PURITY

29

BEFORE THE FALL

Be sure your sin will find you out.[1]

IN THE PACIFIC NORTHWEST, the size and majestic beauty of the elk population has long been a big attraction for hunters and naturalists alike. I have had some great experiences hunting the panhandle of Idaho for bear, and while there have seen some pretty impressive elk herds.

In recent years wildlife managers made the misguided decision to reintroduce the wolf in places like Yellowstone National Park. Wolves brought in from Canada were desired for a more historic representation of animal diversity, but the results have been devastating. In Idaho for example, gray wolves have played a dramatic role in a 20 percent reduction of Idaho's elk herds over the past fifteen years. What's interesting to note is that these wolves don't kill to consume their prey. Hunters in the area find abandoned elk carcasses that have hardly been touched by the wolves that took them down. Wolves often hunt for the thrill of the kill and abandon an elk carcass to scavengers after feeding for only a few minutes.

ANOTHER PREDATOR

Like those wolves, Satan is a serious enemy, described in 1 Peter 5:8 as **"a roaring lion, seeking someone to devour."** In the ancient world the lion was the most feared predator and the one most likely to catch its prey. Men are being stalked by Satan's schemes in the area of sexual sin, and their carcasses litter the landscape. A marriage destroyed, a trust shattered, and a quiver full of children devastated and left alone to comprehend how a man who says he loves God and family could do such things. The word from God's Word about what Satan wants to do to you and me is **"devour."** Satan is taking down men at an alarming rate, for the thrill of the kill. Christian men are especially vulnerable as a real trophy for an enemy that wants most of all to discredit Jesus Christ and make a mockery of those who have taken His name.

KING DAVID GETS DEVOURED

The "man after God's heart,"[2] King David, was not a perfect man. He loved God, modeled a worshipful life, reigned according to God's principles, but couldn't "keep it in his pants." Second Samuel 11 describes David's adultery with Bathsheba.

If you have ever stood in the midst of moral failure and sorted through the wreckage it leaves in its wake, you will have heard the common refrain, "How did this happen?" God's Word reveals through David's infidelity the five steps that get a man where he never planned to go. Trace the steps with me quickly from 2 Samuel 11:1–5 and catch yourself before you crash.

- First step down: Prosperous times produce passive wills. **"In the spring of the year, the time when kings go out to battle . . . But David remained at Jerusalem."** Few of us can handle the temptation of inactivity. By not being where he was supposed to be, David was an easy prey.
- Second step down: Passive wills produce overpowering emotions. **"It happened, late one afternoon, when David arose from his couch and was walking on the roof of the king's house, that he saw from the roof a woman bathing."** He was channel surfing and one look hooked him. With irresistible power, desire seizes mastery of the flesh. And all at once, a secret smoldering fire is kindled.

- Third step down: Overpowering emotions produce perverse thoughts. **"And the woman was very beautiful. And David sent and inquired about the woman. And one said, 'Is not this Bathsheba, the daughter of Eliam, the wife of Uriah the Hittite?'"** Feelings tend to become actions. Forget she was someone's daughter and another man's wife. What the mind desires, the will exercises and goes after.
- Fourth step down: Perverse thoughts produce private sin. **"So David sent messengers and took her, and she came to him, and he lay with her."** When we dwell on desire, yielding is just a matter of time.
- Fifth step down: Private sin produces public consequences. **"And the woman conceived, and she sent and told David, 'I am pregnant.'"** What the rationalizing, deceitful heart says it can avoid, it cannot.

SATANIC SLIPPING

What is clear from David's story is that he did not randomly jump off a cliff one day. It all happened so gradually. I was on the phone yesterday with Johnny Hunt, a pastor friend from Woodstock, Georgia. His church has a residential ministry for pastors in moral failure called City of Refuge. We were talking about a mutual friend who had fallen, who had asked Johnny to relay this message to other men: "You don't realize all that you are giving up in the moment of temptation." It happens so slowly that failure is barely perceptible until you are devoured. I have always loved the following poem by Emily Dickinson. Read it a few times until the warning really clicks for you.

> Crumbling is not an instant's Act
> A fundamental pause
> Dilapidation's processes
> Are organized Decays—

'Tis first a Cobweb on the Soul
A Cuticle of Dust
A Borer in the Axis
An Elemental Rust—

Ruin is formal—Devil's work
Consecutive and slow—
Fail in an instant, no man did
Slipping—is Crashe's law—

"Ruin is formal—Devil's work." Be assured that our enemy wants to devour you. I challenge you to look at your life today and see where there is slippage.

MY JOURNEY TO SEXUAL PURITY (PART 5)

My fear of failing morally began with the falls of some high-profile preachers. Their ministries were far from mine doctrinally, but I did admire the extent to which God used them and was shocked beyond belief when they crashed and burned. More moral failures occurred closer to home: a college professor I admired, a youth pastor I went to college with, and a leader in my home church who trained me in visitation ministry. Like a meteor shower, it seemed that people were cratering all around and my fear of following in their footsteps was real and growing.

I was faithful to my wife, I wasn't addicted to pornography—by that I mean I never sought it out, but sometimes struggled to look away when it seemed to find me. That lack of self-control caused me to fear. What if (unlikely to say the least) someone threw herself at me? Better men than me seemed to be falling like flies and I really battled fear in this area. By the early nineties I was doing my doctoral studies at Denver and Phoenix seminary and chose as my thesis title, "Increasing the Incidents of Self-Disclosure of Sin among Men." In other words, what are men's sin struggles and how can we get them to bring these into the open and deal with them? My fear was driving me to study this area and the work was truly life-changing.

More on that in the final section of this book, but suffice it to say, I have walked further and more deeply into men's sin—and specifically sexual sin—than most people I know who have not struggled significantly themselves. I have sat and listened to men addicted to prostitution, men into crazy perversion, men with low-grade but persistent porn addiction, and men who can't enjoy intimacy with their own wives because of the images corroding their minds. I am not afraid anymore and I am living in victory.

Romans 13:14 has provided a key for me: **"But put on the Lord Jesus Christ, and make no provision for the flesh, to gratify its desires."** Here are three drastic actions that I have lived by now for thirty years, which have been wonderful provisions for a life-giving, healthy marriage. They are very specific examples of making no provision for the flesh:

- No unfiltered access to the Internet
  I have no unfiltered access to the Internet. We use "blockers" that cut off access to certain sites and "tattlers" that send selected friends updates on the sites you're visiting online. The devious mind can find some ways around blockers; there is no way around tattlers because consequences are on the way immediately upon failure.

- Blocked channels on television
  No unblocked channels on our television. My wife has the password to the channels we do get. I don't trust myself with that information. Get your goals right. Down with entertainment; up with obedience to the Lord and living a life that honors Him.

- No unaccountable time
  I don't have one minute a month where people don't know exactly where I am. I have *Covenant Eyes* on my phone. Kathy and I actually

have an app on our smartphones called *Finding Friends*, which allows either of us to find the other at any time.

Making no provision for the flesh means putting barriers between anywhere I know I shouldn't go but might be tempted to go. But more on that in the next study.

QUESTIONS FOR REFLECTION

1. How do you react to the awareness that Satan wants to devour you?

2. Is sexual temptation your greatest exposure to failure or is it something else?

3. What step in David's failure is the most needed warning for your life? Why?

4. Do you have a healthy fear of moral failure? When does it become unhealthy?

5. Where in your life is there "slippage" and what will you do to correct this?

Prayer:

Father,
I praise You today that "greater is He that is in [me] than he that is in the world."[3] *I come to You now, aware of the Enemy that desires to devour, but I pray for the strength to be a man of authenticity for Your glory. Help me always to see what I give up when I allow secret sin to encroach upon my relationship with*

You. Remind me how sin grieves Your Holy Spirit and forfeits the strength You want to express through my life. Help me to live in that today. In Jesus' strong name, amen.

NEXT TIME:

HOW GOD AND DAVID CAME TO TERMS

30

OUR STRONG GOD

*Surely You desire integrity in the inner self,
and You teach me wisdom deep within.*[1]

WHEN WE THINK OF THE PERFECTIONS of our God, those attributes without which He would cease to be God, we tend to think of His holiness, omnipotence, eternality, etc. Interesting, though, how incredibly frequently God the Father is described in terms of His strength!

- Proverbs 18:10, **"The name of the LORD is a strong tower."**
- Psalm 136:12 describes God with a **"strong hand and an outstretched arm."**
- Psalm 144:2 tells us God is loving and a fortress stronghold.
- Isaiah 51:9, **"Awake, awake, put on strength, O arm of the LORD."**
- Psalm 93:1, **"The LORD reigns; he is robed in majesty; the LORD is robed; he has put on strength as his belt."**

Starting from scratch, in just a few minutes I was able to discover all that from an online Bible concordance. This is just a sampling of the river of references in God's revelation of Himself—the Scriptures—regarding

His strength. Notice that God's residence, His arm, His hand, in fact His very clothing is S-T-R-E-N-G-T-H!

STRENGTH FLOWS FROM AUTHENTICITY

God's perfections are unchanging because He is immutable, and enduring because He is eternal. James said, **"With whom there is no variation or shadow due to change."**[2] Among the many attributes of God that never change, that cannot change, is of course His strength. Within the nature of God is a strength that is fashioned in His perfection. Strength flows from the fountain of God's integrity. Honest people are the strongest people. Internally consistent men experience the flow of God's strength. The thesis of this section is that a man cannot experience the strength of the Lord apart from a personal authenticity. The reason so many are battling anxiety, fighting down their fears, wrestling with doubts, and falling into compromise is that they are without God's strength. And the main reason they are without God's strength is because strength is formed in authenticity and that is our greatest lack.

Psalm 51 is the record of David's repentance for adultery and murder. To be repentant you have to change your mind about the lies that led to your sin. David started out believing he could have God *and* his sin, but in the end confessed, **"Surely You desire integrity in the inner self, and You teach me wisdom deep within."**[3]

AUTHENTICITY IS BETTER THAN COVER-UP

In our last study we learned that David was compromising in a lot of little ways before he jumped in bed with another man's wife. David was at home when he should have been at war. David was dwelling on desire until the spark of temptation became an inferno. Once the blaze was raging, his mind found a way to get what in better days he would have run from. This is the David of such integrity that he wouldn't even speak against Saul, the king who was trying to murder him. But how far he had strayed because he allowed himself to live with internal dissonance and thereby forfeited the strength to withstand temptation.

Authenticity is the first thing to go when a man sets out for rock bottom. David's conclusion about God's desire for truth in his innermost being was not arrived at when he woke up in bed with Bathsheba. Sadly, he spent a year running from the truth before he bowed to it, and his running made things so much worse.

Once the consequences for David began to materialize with Bathsheba's pregnancy announcement, his first response was to make a mess messier. It's also the first thing we do when we set out, meaning to or not, to solve rather than face a sin problem. We care more about appearance than reality. David's preoccupying thought should have been, *I am horribly clogged up with sinfulness in my heart. That's the real me.* Instead, David was only concerned about covering up the source of Bathsheba's pregnancy, making it look like everything was fine. He was trying to look like he was doing what God wanted him to do and keeping up appearances. Big mistake. He cared more about appearance than reality.

Here's the second thing David did that we do too. He tried to use others to his benefit even if it hurt them. He recalled Uriah from the front and tried a lame tactic of confusing the paternity of Bathsheba's child by having her husband sleep with her on leave. Uriah had so much integrity he didn't even see the trap or fall in it. If you're in a situation where you've fallen, where you've blown it spiritually, where you're struggling, you will be tempted to care more about what *looks* good than what *is* good, and you will also be tempted to use other people to your benefit even if it hurts them.

Third, David (like us) refused to admit guilt even if it caused more sin. We're making the failure in our life worse as we try to cover it up. We refuse to admit guilt even if it leads to more sin. David took this to the lowest level you can go—he arranged for Uriah's death by sending him back to the war and having General Joab put him on the front lines. Uriah never realizes how he has been betrayed by his wife and his king. But God was watching all of this unfold.

Like David we have a number of self-destructive options we use to avoid repenting and admitting sin. I'll list them and let you come up with personal examples for each: deny, avoid, blame shift, rationalize, and give excuses. If you can't think of how you've used these, you may be stuck in denial!

FENCES FOR GRACE AND PURITY

I explained in the last study how fearful I was about falling morally when I was a young pastor. I remember one afternoon when I had to sit in the tire shop for two hours about a mile from our church office. I called on the pay phone (no cells back then) and told my secretary I was stuck and asked if she could bring me my books and Bible. She offered to pick me up and drive me back to my office but I had pledged myself to something I had decided to call "moral fences." There was no way I was gonna budge. Even though she is closer to my mom's age than mine and a saint in the truest sense, I told her no and just sat there. Seems kind of crazy now, but I am thankful I put some rules in place to serve as guardrails against sin that could destroy my calling as a pastor. A moral fence is a decision to forgo a particular behavior that though not wrong could lead to a wrong or a wrong appearance. Every man I have ever known who fell morally started down by crossing one of these lines. By establishing them as hard-and-fast rules I won't break, I set in place a warning system for those around me to alert them to decay in my heart before it would become visible. Here are those moral fences:

- I will not, under any circumstances, ride alone in a car with a female other than my wife or an immediate family member.
- I do not counsel a woman in a closed room or more than once.
- I do not stay alone in a hotel overnight.
- I speak often and publicly of my affection for my wife, when she's present and when she's not.
- I compliment the character or the conduct, not the coiffure or the clothing.

There is a specific rationale behind each of these. While they protect those in ministry, they can certainly be a standard practice for any godly man.

Some have criticized these moral standards as too legalistic or too narrow. But they are not legalism unless you judge others for not following them. Ignoring one or more of them doesn't immediately lead to a fall, but it moves you closer to the edge. They are my rules, and the pastors in our church have agreed to follow them too. Through the years they have provided a great protection for us. Of course, no set of rules can keep a bad intentioned man with hypocrisy in his heart from immorality, but these rules are not designed to stop men determined to do evil, they are to protect and guide men who do **"desire integrity in the inner self."** David got back there eventually but he shouldn't have left and never fully recovered.

QUESTIONS FOR REFLECTION

1. Do you agree that unconfessed sin forfeits God's strength in our lives? Why or why not?

2. What sin have you covered rather than confess? Confess it now.

3. What temptation threatens your authenticity that needs radical removal?

Prayer:

Father,
Thank You for providing David both as a model and warning in Your Word. For all his great qualities, he was not immune from temptation and miserable failure. Help me identify the moral fences I need to honor and lead me to others who can encourage me to keep them. I know the grass will immediately look greener on the other side of any fence, but remind me that it covers the edge of a cliff I don't want to fall off. Thank You for

the abundance of encouragement You have provided and Your promise of being with me every moment. Keep me from ever ignoring Your Spirit's guidance away from sin. In Jesus' name I pray, amen.

NEXT TIME:

A LOOK AT JESUS, WHO IS OUR STRENGTH

31

BACK TO REPENTANCE

*For godly grief produces a repentance
that leads to salvation without regret,
whereas worldly grief produces death.*[1]

IT'S GOING ON IN HEAVEN RIGHT NOW. The unceasing adoration of Jesus Christ by the angels before the throne of God. Talk about tongue-tied! Think of the infinite variety of adjectives that could flow from the lips of cherubim as they hover in place, wings blazing, calling out in unison their worshipful description of the Lamb, Jesus Christ. Holy, worthy, eternal, glorious, loving, infinite, mysterious, majestic, awesome, omniscient, omnipotent, omnipresent, wondrous, beautiful, patient, kind, compassionate, gentle, tender, merciful, just. As one preacher put it, "He is the superlative of everything good that you would choose to call Him. He stands in the solitude of Himself, unparalleled, unprecedented. The greatest phenomena to ever cross the horizon of this world." Paul said, **"Oh, the depth of the riches both of the wisdom and knowledge of God! How unsearchable are His judgments and His ways past finding out!"**[2]

STRENGTH AND POWER

Given that eternity will not exhaust the excellencies of the Savior, it's very instructive to note the words that are used in the heavenly chorus that never ends. I would doubt the angels made it up themselves. My guess is that God Himself chose the summary words that would encapsulate the infinite. In Revelation 5:12 we see remarkably that strength made the short list. Other throne-room verses use some of these words, but this verse uses seven descriptors for the indescribable holiness of the Lord: power, wealth, wisdom, strength (NIV), honor, glory, blessing. Some versions translate it as "might," but what's significant is that two of the seven main attributes, power and strength, have to do with the Lord's infinite, inexhaustible capacity to accomplish all that needs doing. Or as Isaiah basically put it, **"The everlasting God does not grow weary or tired, and by waiting on Him we can renew our strength."**[3] When we wait on the Lord, we invite Him to root out the dissonance in a divided heart and bring to us the integrity of full surrender to His will. In that we experience His strength.

JESUS PERSONIFIES STRENGTH

I hate the false notion that Jesus Christ was weak. "Oh poor Jesus, out in the cold, knocking at the door of your heart, let Him in, let Him in." That kind of preaching is pathetic and flies in the face of the biblical portrait of Christ. Yes, He was tenderhearted to those in need, but He was brutal on religious blockheads, and He was absolutely the opposite of wimpy. Jesus walked out of a temple after flipping over the trade tables of the religious hypocrites, sending their coins clanking and their tempers rising. They wanted to kill Him but the Scripture says no one dared to touch Him. He stood in a circle of men holding rocks ready to stone the lust out of a near naked woman. As He wrote in the sand waiting for someone to throw the first pitch, they walked away one by one. You wouldn't want to mess with Jesus Christ. Jesus fasted for forty days and nights in the wilderness yet stood up to satanic attack without yielding on a single point. He commanded great crowds and stood fearless in the face of opposition from fierce storms and from false accusers. Jesus Christ was strong, immensely strong. Not "I'm gonna beat your brains in, meathead!" strong, but **"No one takes it** [my life] **from Me . . . I have power to lay it down, and I have power to take it again"**[4] strong.

Jesus Christ was full deity (God) dwelling in undiminished humanity. Hebrews 4:15 tells us that He was **"in all points tempted as we are, yet without sin."** Bible scholars call this the impeccability of Jesus, the fact that He was without sin and could not sin. His humanity could be tempted by sin but His deity would not allow the God/Man to choose it. This is the secret to His strength. People used to watch Samson and they couldn't figure out his strength, but we know from Scripture that his strength was in his authentic obedience to God; when one left, the other did too. Jesus personifies the strength that comes with full obedience and an undivided authentic heart. Sadly Samson personifies the opposite.

REPENT TO EXPERIENCE STRENGTH

If you haven't noticed, most of our lessons end with a prayer for forgiveness. This is where the strength begins to flow again. God's grace **"cleanses us from all unrighteousness" "if we confess our sins."**[5] The word *confession* actually means to "say what God says." The problem is that we can't truly say what God says about our sin until we see what God sees. Most guys trapped in an endless cycle of "sin confess, sin confess, sin confess" begin to wonder if they will ever see progress and stop stumbling in the same old spots. The answer is yes, you can see change, but the word you need is *repentance*. Confession follows repentance. You can't say what God says about your sin until you see it as God sees it. That is the purpose of repentance. Sadly, it's a word that has fallen on hard times, and the loss of preaching repentance is why we as men have such a difficult time getting past certain temptations.

Repent was the one-word sermon repeated by every Old Testament prophet. They would show up to deliver a message and say, "Good morning . . . *repent!* . . . let's pray." Their approach was right to the point, and their message and method moved God's people. The New Testament times might have been a new day, but the first preacher up to bat, John the Baptist, delivered his message: **"Repent, for the kingdom of heaven is at hand."**[6] He was followed by Jesus Christ Himself, who began His public ministry by saying, **"Repent, for the kingdom of heaven is at hand."**[7] Then the apostles echoed the same urgent message: repent! There was one consistent theme of preaching in the New Testament: repentance.

So how do you know when your recognition of sin in your own life reaches the level called repentance? Here, briefly, are five marks of genuine repentance:

- Grief over sin: Repentance is at work when your awareness of sin causes deep pain, sorrow, and shame with no hints of excuse or blaming of others. You relate to the unworthiness experienced by people who encountered the holiness of God.
- Repulsion over my sin: Repentance is at work when shame is joined by sickening and pulling back from sin as filthy, ugly, and contagious no matter how attractive it was in the past.
- Restitution toward others: Repentance is at work when sin has harmed others and it results in urgent action to make things right even at great cost.
- Revival toward God: Repentance is at work when God's open arms are run to without hesitation, like a child after loving punishment, eager to be back in fellowship. A healthy fear of God and of sinning further develops.
- Moving forward: Repentance is at work when you get locked in on what's ahead and experience freedom from what's behind.

GROWING IN GRACE AND PERSONAL PURITY

Repentance was the difference maker for me. I had never fully understood what it means to repent. Back in 2000 when I was finishing the Moody Publishers book now titled *Lord Change Me*, I had to come face-to-face with my own need for repentance. No exceptions, no secret corners of struggle, no semiannual stumblings in what I set before my eyes. I can't say I have batted 1000 since God did the work of deep repentance in my heart, but I can say with total authenticity that I never saw the sin of lust the same way again. What sometimes roused me as a young man now repulses me. What once stirred me now sickens me. I detected and destroyed the lie that the most fulfilling sexuality was outside my marriage, and by God's grace I am walking in that victory. If you are not yet walking in victory, you truly can. It starts with genuine repentance.

QUESTIONS FOR REFLECTION

1. What is the connection between authenticity and strength? How did Samson lose it, and why didn't Jesus?

2. Describe the time in your life you experienced personal repentance most deeply. What have been the long-term results?

3. What prevents you from turning to God and asking Him to give you true repentance wherever it is needed right now?

Prayer:

Lord,
Thank You for changing my heart. You have produced such a deep grief in me over what I've done. I have excused the inexcusable and blamed others for my wrongdoing. I see that as sin now and am turning around. As best as I know how, I'm repenting of all the things that have kept me dry and distant from You. It makes me sick just to think of how I've allowed this to linger in my life.

But by Your grace I am dealing with it now. Already I sense that You are welling up in me the hope of restoration and the rightness of reconciliation to You. Don't stop, Lord! I am stepping out in faith, performing deeds in keeping with repentance. Thank You for this renewed season of mercy to get this work done. I'm getting on the right road and not looking back. This I pray in Jesus' name, amen.

NEXT TIME:

THE HOLY SPIRIT AND STRENGTH

32

LETTING YOUR PARTNER LEAD

*For all who are led by the
Spirit of God are sons of God.*[1]

THE MOST UNCOMFORTABLE I HAVE EVER been is a toss-up between two memorable chasms of exhausting awkwardness. I grew up in a family of four boys, not a girl in sight. For this reason my daughter had to suffer through the complete confusion I feel about fancy dresses, foofy food, and worst of all (drumroll please)—dancing. I was absolutely worn out with fearful anticipation of dancing in front of a roomful of dads and looking like a dork. No problem checking my ego; I never considered skipping, I wouldn't do that to my little girl. I just knew I was gonna fall on my face and wanted to get it over with. We got to school for the Daddy/ Daughter dance, and honestly, I couldn't have been prouder of my adorable kid, feeling exceedingly happy to be seen with her. As we walked into the crowded gym, the *Jaws* movie sound track was playing in my mind and growing louder: dunt, duh, dunt, duh, dunt, duh . . . In moments I knew I would be standing in shame staring into the eyes of my little princess as she learned that her daddy was a dancing dunce while others tittered with amusement at the big buffoon. As luck would have it, right beside us was some Fred Astaire who took the house down with pirouettes and a waltz fox-trot thingamajig. It was so exhausting to feel so out of place even as I was doing the job that fathers do.

I broke into a sweat typing that even though it's almost twenty years ago now and my Abby only mentions it occasionally. The other time I got crushed by awkwardness was the time I was invited and inexplicably agreed to speak to more than six thousand women for Nancy Leigh DeMoss's True Woman event in Fort Worth, Texas. I got there late and stumbled into the backstage room to be greeted by a group of huggy women and a table of sandwiches and fruit that shouted, "You're in the wrong place, buddy." As women stared at my obvious discomfort, I searched the room for another male like a kid fresh out of fat camp looks for a Twinkie. I was so very uncomfortable and it was so exhausting. I don't remember how many people I offended in my stumbling efforts at humor and audience connection, but I know, in spite of the worthy ministry and wonderful hospitality, I literally could not wait to spur my horse and ride outta Fort Worth.

IT'S MORE THAN WEARING THE UNIFORM

As men we are forced into many situations in our roles as provider, protector, father, husband, and pastor to our families. Too often we skip training and just stumble along in our roles, wearing the right uniform but having no clue how to get over the hump and actually fulfill the role effectively. That awkwardness, more than anything else, leads to exhaustion. I could direct you to a lot of places to find helpful insight on what to do in the various roles, but I think the larger issue is the complete and total drain of energy that follows every time we just fake it. Had I planned ahead and prepared for my daughter's dance by practicing, I would have been chomping at the bit to get to the school gym. The exhaustion was the result of being outside what I really knew how to do. I don't think we will ever have enough information to avoid the inevitable "fish out of water" uncertainty or exhaustion. What we need as men is a source of strength outside ourselves. We have been studying what that strength is and where it's found, how secret sin forfeits God's blessing and drains that strength.

STRENGTH ON THE WAY

The Holy Spirit was sent into the world to convict. John 16:8 says, **"And when he comes** (the Helper, the Advocate, the Counselor, and the Comforter—the Holy Spirit), **he will convict."** Now there is a word you haven't heard for a long time—convict. That's a great word. Here's a little definition. Convict: to expose; to bring to light; to uncover what is hidden; evidence that cannot be refuted; shown to be guilty; verdict supplied and applied. Convicted!

We love the part about the Holy Spirit as a Comforter, but can't we just skip the part about Him being the Convictor?

No, we cannot! We must welcome His conviction as a man in a burning building welcomes the firefighter. By convicting us, the Holy Spirit presses us to deal with the things that become hindrances to the rest of His ministry in our lives.

Jesus promised in John 16:8, **"And when he comes, he will convict the world concerning** (here are the three things) **sin** (what's wrong) **and righteousness** (what's right) **and judgment** (why you need to take care of this)."

The Holy Spirit convicts us of the wrong: *Don't do that.* And of the right: *Do this instead.* And then the result: *You're going to answer to God about this, so pay attention and keep your focus.* Unless we are tuned in and willing to listen to the Holy Spirit's prompts and direction, we will be as hopelessly unprepared for real-life challenges as I was in facing the daunting Daddy/Daughter dance with so much more on the line.

WHAT AN AWFUL FEELING

It was before 6:00 a.m. and I normally sleep 'til after 7:00 a.m. on Sunday mornings. I awoke with a start and a pit in my stomach that signaled to me something was wrong, maybe. My oldest son, Luke, tracks things in and outside our church very closely, but he texted back quickly to say all was well. I went downstairs and found Kathy, who could think of no reason on a sunny Sunday morning that I would not wake up rejoicing. Then I checked Twitter. It didn't take long. One of my dearest friends in ministry was caught in moral failure and lost his position in disgrace. The details were unspeakably shameful, and I sat in my chair and wept for an hour. Then I felt anger over his selfishness and irresponsibility. Worse, I grieved that so many who had trusted and followed his leadership would be devastated.

Of this you can be sure: at the point of temptation, the Holy Spirit was screaming for a halt to his tragic trajectory. When failures become big and public, they seem sudden to the outsider, but secretly they have been coming for a long time. Way before you shut down the Holy Spirit's conviction with gross immorality or other devastating sin, you have become very proficient at ignoring His voice in your life. Ephesians 4:30 instructs us, **"Do not grieve the Holy Spirit,"** which we do whenever we take action that He has been protesting in our hearts by causing us pause and a strong sense of foreboding. First Thessalonians 5:19 commands, **"Do not quench the Spirit,"** which we do when we refuse the Holy Spirit's provocation to action when He repeatedly presents and reminds us of something we know needs doing. For example, if you had negative and unnecessary conflict with someone in your family, the Holy Spirit is grieved when you sin against those you love and quenched when you don't go back to humble yourself with a sincere apology. Over time the voice of the Holy Spirit becomes more and more muted in your life until you can callously choose a course of action that in better days you would have believed impossible.

Don't be overwhelmed over the pressure of countless life choices. The Holy Spirit lives inside you to lead you moment by moment into obedience to God's Word. **"As many as are led by the Spirit of God, these are sons of God."**[2] His convicting presence in your life and mine is our very best opportunity to live quality lives and truly act like the men God has called us to be. Let your partner take the lead.

QUESTIONS FOR REFLECTION

1. How do you sense the ministry of the Holy Spirit in your life, convicting you of right and wrong and your accountability to God?

2. What advantages do you see in the ministry of the Holy Spirit that would lead you to welcome and prayerfully invite a fuller experience of His work?

3. What wrong in action or attitude may have grieved or even quenched the Holy Spirit that you could repent of?

Prayer:

Dear Holy Spirit of God,
Please forgive my wayward heart that thinks about and chooses what I know must grieve You. Please forgive the times You have convicted me to show humility and seek unity but I have stubbornly resisted and been prideful. I ask You now to take renewed leadership of my life and direct me according to Your Word, even through this study, into a much deeper and more consistent expression of what You created man to be. For Jesus' sake I pray, amen.

NEXT TIME:
WHEN MEN FIGURE OUT THAT LOVE IS MISSING

DO EVERYTHING IN

LOVE

33

DOING IT
ALL IN LOVE?

Let love be without hypocrisy.[1]

WERE YOU HATEFUL AS A KID? For me, **"Let all that you do be done in love"**[2] was sadly not even on my radar. I was taught to obey God but somehow missed the lesson that "LOVE is the fulfillment of the law."[3] I have memories both of being hateful and being the one hated—tough stuff to be sure.

From our earliest memories we compare stature and appearance, our intellect, athleticism, and internal fortitude to the men around us. We strain for signs that we are accepted in the pack, and as I remember it, we were pretty hard on kids we considered to be falling behind in any area. I recall with shame two kids in our elementary school. One was from an impoverished family living in a rented home on the edge of our suburb. Kids would egg his house and punch him when he wasn't looking. When he walked by, girls would shriek and jump up on the coatrack benches as though he were a monster in a horror flick and their feet couldn't touch the floor at the same time as his. Everyone called him by his hardly subtle nickname "Scum." I would empty my savings to find him today and tell him how sorry I am for being too afraid of others to obey my conscience and stand with a kid so often standing alone.

The other guy I remember had a disability that bent his legs at obtuse angles and could barely support his tiny frame even with the assistance of crutches. His head was slightly misshapen and most kids alternated between calling him "Hammer Head" and "Puss." I am so ashamed as I write these words and pray that God has healed these men of the scars left by insecure kids who chose attacking others as the way to entrench and defend their personal feelings of inadequacy. We were stupid, insecure kids who needed a good beating from someone willing to stand up to our brazenness. We spent our energies making others feel small because that made our darkened hearts feel better about self. We were the furthest thing from quality men who live with urgency and clarity in God's strength. We exhausted ourselves by being idiots who should have known better but didn't. Where were the men in our lives who knew what it was to act like a man?

Wouldn't it be great if attacking others to feel better about ourselves was something we outgrew like acne or crying when we have to go to bed? The fact is, many men still exhaust themselves in critiquing and attacking others. Maybe we fear that other people's success will somehow diminish ours. Maybe we take responsibility for more than we really need to and have appointed ourselves protectors of some kingdom. Deeper down, though, men are driven to stand in judgment of others because we have a *deeply engrained bent* and a pesky, persistent pattern of seeming to be wise in our own eyes. This makes love an impossibility.

BOTTOM LINE: LOVE

"All scripture is God-breathed,"[4] and **"Holy men of God spoke as they were moved by the Holy Spirit."**[5] This is why we understand that when the Holy Spirit spoke 1 Corinthians 16:13–14 into the heart and mind of the apostle Paul, we were getting the very heart of God about what men were made to do. We know we are called to act like quality men with urgency that is governed by clarity in the strength of the Lord. What remains is this matter of love. Or as Paul put it, **"Let all that you do be**

done in love."[6] He had us men in the crosshairs.

Keep in mind that Paul has already penned the definition of love in 1 Corinthians 13. If you are like me, you have sat through countless weddings and heard, **"If I speak in the tongues of men and of angels, but have not love . . . I am nothing. . . . Love is patient and kind; love does not envy or boast . . . ,"** etc. By the time the bridesmaid is halfway through reading, your eyes glaze over like you just ate half a dozen Krispy Kremes and you start to think, "Man, that is just way too much, nobody can love like that!"

Don't let the poetic nature of Scripture's definition of love put you in the ditch. Please don't let the wedding context where you hear that most frequently give you the false notion that biblical love is romantic and decorated with lace and fine china. We have to take love back from Hallmark cards and the Lifetime Network. Love should not be hijacked by the romantics. Men need to know that you don't need to become a woman to love others as God designed for the benefit of all.

If you are like most men, the poetry can derail rather than expand your understanding. I know I always appreciate content that gets boiled down, so let me give you the bottom line. Love is selfless! Love is "you before me" decision making. Need it shorter? Love = Ub4me! There it is.

BIBLICAL MASCULINE LOVE

I believe masculinity at its best has created some of the most inspirational examples of real love in human history. Eric and Brian were among the first Marines sent into Iraq during the first Gulf War. They also ended up being the first two casualties. Eric was a twelve-year staff sergeant and Brian was a newly assigned medical corpsman. Both were from Texas but they met and became friends in Kuwait as they trained among younger men (Eric was 33; Brian 29).

In one of the tragedies that multiply in war, during a rest stop in the desert, Eric stepped on a land mine. Without hesitating, Brian went to his aid, little knowing as he feverishly worked to control his friend's bleeding that he was kneeling on another land mine himself. When he moved, it went off, injuring him even worse than Eric's wounds. They were med-evacuated and began a series of emergency medical interventions, though both men eventually lost a leg.

During the extensive recovery and therapy period back in the States, the two friends encouraged each other. Eric told Brian at least once how bad he felt that his injury had led to his friend's, but his buddy waved it off with, "I was just doing my job."

A year later, they were both able to go skiing at a disabled event in Colorado, the culmination of a long road of rehabilitation. The friendship that began as fellow marines has been strengthened as they suffered and recovered together.

The words **let-all-that-you-do-be-done-in-love** speak for them-selves. Selfless, sacrificial, you-before-me living. Not hard to understand but incredibly difficult to apply in actual life situations.

LEARNING TO LOVE

A pastor gets told that he is loved by a lot of people in a lot of situa-tions; sadly though, it often is not true in the biblical sense. Sometimes what others really mean is "I love what you do for me." Nothing sacrificial about that. Other times they mean, "I love being close to you and how that makes me feel," which is fine until they lose proximity, and what they called love evaporates like a puddle in the sun. Worst of all is the "I love you, Pastor," which means, "I love who I think you are from listening to your sermons," and you fear what will happen when they discover that pastors are just people too and struggle along with everyone else. Yes, let's change the subject to my failures to love.

I became a pastor not because I loved people per se but because I loved the truth and how it impacted people. I loved my friends, I love my family immensely, but I didn't have a love for humanity. I didn't love the stranger at the mall or the stinker in my church. I practiced a conditional, nonsacrificial kind of love. I loved the church member who attended, served, listened, and grew but didn't make an already impossible job harder. When people became an obstacle instead of assisting in building a Christ-honoring church, I would move toward them but not in love. Instead, I had this bizarre way of trying to control/influence them so the threat of their contrary, critical, constantly constipated and complaining conduct could be contained or crushed. The worst part was the crushing. When I couldn't figure a way to put that kind of person out of my misery, exhausted by the energy drain of managing their downside, I came on way too strong and hurt them while helping them off the train. In my mind I justified the removal of impediments to worthy goals, the elimination of threats to a fruitful ministry, the reduction of downside so the upside could flourish. The problem with all that was accepting any goal as worthy, any fruit as biblical, or any upside as truly advancing the cause of Jesus that didn't begin and end with love. I was wrong, totally wrong, and had to come to the place where I grieved the failure to love as the greatest failure a Christian is capable of.

QUESTIONS FOR REFLECTION

1. What events in your past present a challenge of shame or regrets when you think about practicing love now?

2. When you think about the ways a man can authentically love, what things come to mind?

3. Who has been your best model for loving in a manly way? Why?

Prayer:

Father,
When I read the accounts of Your Son's relationship with His disciples, I can't help but be drawn to the way He loved them. He was blunt, honest, correcting, and sometimes angry but always loving. I want to be like that. I know He reflected in a human way the love that You have for me and everyone I know.

I know when You command me to love, You are not giving me permission to love in my limited capacity but to let You love through me. I confess that most days I can hardly think about what that means, but with Your indwelling help I want to do better. Thank You for the hope I get from the patience You give me. Teach me to love like Your Son. In His name I pray, amen.

NEXT TIME:
WHY EVERYTHING SHOULD BE
DONE IN LOVE

34

LOVE HAS A LOT TO DO WITH IT

Greater love has no one than this,
that someone lay down his life for his friends.[1]

"LET ALL THAT YOU DO BE DONE IN LOVE"[2] doesn't leave a ton of wiggle room does it? If you take the biblical command seriously and reflect on the many choices you have made as a man, maybe you feel as overwhelmed as I do. All that I do . . . at home, at work, at play, in traffic, at the drive-through window, when the garage mechanic is lying to me, when the friend is betraying me, when the fallout from other people's failed performance is piling up on me, when my kids are screaming and my wife is crying and my heart is breaking . . . God's Word is reaching past my rationalizations and demanding . . . **"let all that you do be done in love."**

And not just in particular times or seasons of life, or in awful circumstances, but in every doing: doing my job, doing what my wife asked, doing what needs to be done, doing my own thing, doing the right thing, doing time, doing "that thing you do," or in choosing to do nothing, which is also a something of a different sort that doesn't exempt me from the "no wiggle room" of **"let all that you do be done in love."** No matter the place or time or circumstance of my action or inaction, the decisive factor in its worthiness before God, the final filter in the deciding if it's "a go," is the love test. No matter what, when, who, how, or why, if it's not loving, it's a total fail. Get this right and no matter what is wrong, I am part of the solution. Get this wrong and no matter how much I care, how hard I try, how many excuses I muster for why I didn't do better, I can't say I don't know anymore . . . all things, done, in, love.

This poem/hymn entitled "Love Is the Theme" by Albert C. Fisher captures the sense of the love we're after:

> Of the themes that men have known
> One Uniquely Stands alone
> Love is the theme, love is Supreme!
> Sweeter it grows, glory bestows, bright as the sun, ever it glows.
> Love is the theme, the Eternal theme.

THE ONLY THING

We have all heard it said, "The main thing is that you keep the main thing the main thing," but the main thing in following Jesus is such a big thing that by comparison to the small things, it's the *only thing*. I used to think of love as a main thing, a top-five thing, maybe top three, but as something that had to be set aside if necessary when truth was on the line. Nope. The Bible helps us with that when it says, **"Speaking the truth in love."**[3] Then, as God began to shape me through trial and error, I thought I was walking in big-time victory if I wore my love filter and didn't do anything that didn't pass through the grid of "is this loving?" But that's not it either.

Love is not a governor on the engine of anything else. My final upgrade was when I thought that love was a means to a higher end. Be loving in conflict or be loving in frustration or let love command your every interaction because **"love never fails."**[4] Yes, love never fails to accomplish God's purpose, but again, love is not a means to an end, love is not a way to win or the way to get to something else, because there *is* nothing else—love is the thing. Love is the goal, beginning and end of the law, the first and last priority—the proof of true conversion, the evidence to the world that we follow Christ. And most interesting of all for this study on biblical manhood, according to Jesus, one man's sacrificial love for a friend is the summa cum laude pinnacle of it all: **"Greater love has no one than this, *that someone lay down his life for his friends."*[5]** This is what Jesus Christ did for us and commands that we do for one another. Interesting that a failure to do this increasingly is also evidence of the opposite: **"If anyone says, 'I love God,' and hates his brother, he is a liar."[6]**

LOVE IS MANLY

To really act like a man, you have to be willing to set aside your crazy thoughts of love as a theme for date-night movies, and pleas of "I thought you said you love me" as a way for a woman to get what she wants after you used the words to get what you want. Without question, the greatest thing has been used and abused by us all, but experience with a counterfeit is no reason to swear off the original.

God has established love and modeled love and created us to need it. Not sex, love. Men need unselfish, brothers first, you-before-me love. So many men are broken because they didn't have it in their father, didn't find it in their work, don't appreciate or cultivate it in their home, and struggle to even admit it's missing. Men need the strength and security of relationships with other Christians. We have to have friendships that are biblical as a method, mutual as an expression, confidential as a mandate, and absolutely totally committed as a prognosis.

Years ago I read a book describing the powerful things that happen when men truly sell out to committed, men with men, community. I have stained the pages of my journal with the tears of failing to live up to this and experiencing the same in the failure of others. I keep returning to it:

Absolute Total Commitment. I want you to know that I'm committed to you. You will never knowingly suffer at my hands. I will never say anything or do anything knowingly to hurt you, even if you hurt me.

I will always, in every circumstance, seek to help and support you. If you're down and I can lift you, I'll do that. If you need something and I have it, I'll share it with you. If need be, I'll give it to you. No matter what I find out about you, no matter what happens in the future— good or bad—my commitment to you will never change and there's nothing you can do about that. You don't have to respond to what I'm saying. I love you and that's what it means. I'm absolutely, totally committed to you.[7]

I'm not using the word *fellowship* here, because it has become so laden with misunderstanding. A lot of people have given up on fellowship because it's used to mean red punch in the church basement after the service. Or stupid games with people you hardly know called "crowd breakers" that make you want to break something! I am using the word *community*. Community for our purposes is men meeting together to support and encourage one another in what it means to act like a man. Some of my greatest life moments have been times of true community with other men. And my greatest heartaches have been in the realization that for no acceptable reason, we gave up on community and failed. We might call it other things but God doesn't bail on us, and when we bail on each other it can't be sugarcoated or explained away. It's a failure to do what never fails, a failure to love.

Meeting with men for mutual community may involve a hobby or a game, it may involve the outdoors or basement workshop or an annual trip. It can gather around a ton of activities, but it always involves real biblical community between men where the Word is studied, hearts are opened, and heads bow in prayer for one another. And hear this: I have never known a man to go the distance for God and family who didn't have this kind of men-with-men, caring Christian community. If you don't have it, you're not going to make it. If you had it and lost it, you need to get it back. If you've never had it or don't know how, the rest of this book will help. The goal of acting like a man is just a pipe dream if you're trying to go it alone, **"for we are members one of another."**[8]

QUESTIONS FOR REFLECTION

1. Describe the best guy friendship you have ever had and what made it so.

2. When was the last time you had a heart-to-heart, mutually disclosing trusted conversation with a friend without fear of fallout or freak out?

3. What makes it hardest for you to find and maintain life-giving friendships?

Prayer:

Dear God,
Thank You for arresting my attention to the priority You place on love. Thank You for showing me that it is not an element or an add-on but the actual purpose of my life and proof of my faith. Thank You for demonstrating Your love to me in Christ dying for my forgiveness while I was yet a sinner. I ask for a deeper and more consistent demonstration of love through my life. Help me especially to love the people in my life most difficult to love and direct my steps into supportive friendships that can work with me to these worthy ends for Your glory. In Jesus' name, amen.

NEXT TIME:
HOW OLD TESTAMENT GUYS MISSED OUT ON COMMUNITY

35

TWO OR MORE ARE MORE

And though a man might prevail against one who is alone, two will withstand him—a threefold cord is not quickly broken.[1]

MY SONS LUKE AND LANDON HAVE a favorite childhood story from a time we were parked just outside Blockbuster (remember those places where you rented videos?). Inside was a guy, let's call him George, who hung around our church a bit, but mostly got drunk and terrorized his former wife. He had been a neighbor of ours, and we were frequently drawn into drama while attempting to help with his destructive behavior. At the time, he was stalking his wife, who had an order of protection for his threatening behavior. It was all pretty sad. Desperate to cause the woman he married pain as payback for what he was feeling, he vengefully dumped sugar into her gas tank so her car wouldn't run. The boys were too young to know better and thought this alleged action by the "red-faced man" known for insanity was humorous.

I can't resist making my kids smile, so we waited for George to come out of the store and when he did, he was startled to see his former neighbor leap out of the car as he approached. I instinctively placed my hands over the gas tank cover and said, "Keep walking, George, just keep walking!" Nothing else needed to be said, because he knew I knew and he didn't even bother to deny ruining his wife's car. He just kept walking as my boys howled inside the car. It's such a funny memory. More than that, a direct confrontation about a cowardly action toward the wife he had promised to love and cherish.

I was at his wedding and heard him tell the Lord what he would do and for how long. In the end, he kept none of his promises to God or wife. He did not in any sense act like a man. He was not quality. He spent his misplaced urgency believing that by causing others pain, he would feel relief from his own. He embezzled from his mother, lied to his friends, and neglected his kids. If you tried to help him, which I did many times, he might listen, but **"like a man who looks intently at his natural face in a mirror,"**[2] he would immediately forget what he had been shown when he walked away.

You might think that the worst flaw in George's life was his very low impulse control or his destructive neglect of family, but what I observed about him through the years, more than anything, was that he was alone. So many people tried to befriend him, but he always inevitably rejected friendship as a threat to his personal autonomy. If you see a man making a mess of his life, acting irrationally and spiraling out of control, you can be sure that man has become isolated. He may have some drinking buddies or friends he hunts with, but nobody is exposing his stinking thinking to the light of rational behavior or biblical truth. If they tried, he cut them off. The crises of a man's life that get everyone's attention only reveal a deterioration that has been happening for a long time. One of the earliest warning signs is isolation.

ISOLATION LEADS TO INSANITY

The stories of Bible men who rejected the need for community with other men and went off the deep end in isolation are brimming from the Bible's pages. It's hard to know which ones to pick:

- Saul was going cuckoo in a cave *by himself,* convinced that David wanted his throne.[3]
- Jonah waited under a withered bush *by himself,* angry with God and begging to die.[4]
- Samson was always *by himself,* unless he was killing, arguing, or having sex.[5]
- Elijah was *by himself,* calling down fire on false prophets, then hiding from a woman.[6]
- Despite their presence as he sat on the ash heap, Job seems to have thought it would be better to suffer in silence *by himself* than sit with his **"miserable comforters."**[7]

How much different would these sad stories have ended if these men hadn't stubbornly insisted on isolating themselves?

Saul would not have gone crazy if he'd just turned to a trusted friend with the courage to expose the folly of his thinking. My guess? He didn't have one. In better times and under the pressure of all his responsibilities, he thought that community with other men was a luxury and it didn't make his short list. Would you have guessed at the time that Saul would end up committing suicide?[8]

Jonah wouldn't have ended up under a desert plant whining narcissistically, **"It is better for me to die than to live."**[9] Isolation was a life pattern for Jonah. He ran from God alone, hung out on a boat with strangers who reluctantly threw him overboard, spent time inside a fish alone, and preached to Nineveh alone. There must have been people from the recent revival offering to accompany Jonah on his wilderness retreat. But when you are planning a pity party, you can't chance somebody showing up with cupcakes, so Jonah took off on his own. Of course God went after Jonah, inquiring gently, **"Do you do well to be angry?"**[10] However, insane from isolation, Jonah answers remarkably, **"Yes, I do well to be angry, angry enough to die."**[11] Wow!

Samson was called by God to lead and fight but totally segregated himself from his countrymen. He worked alone, traveled alone, and was relationally despicable in every instance. He argued with his parents, rejecting their marriage counsel with vocal demands about the woman he wanted.[12] Later, the crowd assigns **"thirty companions to be with him"**[13] because clearly he had no friends of his own. Samson makes them a bet about an impossible riddle, calls his wife a "heifer," and kills thirty other men to pay off his lost bet, while his "best man" runs away with his wife. That's just one chapter in the biblical account of Samson and it gets worse after that. Samson was a slave long before they poked his eyes out—enslaved by the sinful habits he cultivated in isolation.

Elijah, honestly, was a pretty amazing guy, but like most prophetic personalities, not superintuitive relationally. He calls down fire from heaven to kill a boatload of false prophets but can't stand up to one woman named Jezebel who really has his number. So he seeks seclusion in the southern Judea wilderness. To escape the crazy woman, he **"went a day's journey into the wilderness"**[14] and quarantined under shrub, Elijah says, **"It is enough; now, O Lord, take away my life."**[15] Next he walks alone for forty days to "Ten Commandment mountain,"[16] and ends up sequestered in a cave where the Lord shows up to say, **"What are you doing here, Elijah?"**[17] Men get crazy in isolation.

Job has the unique distinction of being a guy God bragged about. **"Have you considered my servant Job, that there is none like him on the earth, a blameless and upright man, who fears God and turns away from evil?"**[18] The problem is that when you're the only guy who fears God, your only option is awful friends. When God allows Job to be tested by suffering, his wife tells him to **"curse God and die,"**[19] and his friends show up as he sits alone in grief and tell him it's his fault. In the end, Job is more harmed than helped by his **"miserable comforters."**[20] How much lighter Job's tough road would have been with biblical community and men around him committed to **"let all that you do be done in love."**[21]

QUALITY MEN

Quickly contrast the stories of these men who never had big downturns, never wavered, wallowed, or walked away from the Lord . . . Daniel had three friends—Shadrach, Meshach, Abednego—and together they stood for God in an evil land under a wicked king.[22] Joshua had Caleb and together they rejected the report of the faithless spies. Standing on the Word of the Lord, they got their families home while the rest of their generation died.[23] Abraham had Lot,[24] Moses had Aaron[25] and Jethro,[26] and David had Jonathan.[27] Strong men serving together thrive in the strength their friendship provides. Isolated men struggle with circumstances and themselves because they have no one to arrest their attention when they get off course, and no one to call them out when they are out of line. Are you like David and Daniel? Or are you like Jonah and Job?

QUESTIONS FOR REFLECTION

1. Name your three closest friends and a time they called you out and held you accountable.

2. When was a time you felt most alone and how did it negatively impact what you were facing?

3. What man do you know personally who best exemplifies the importance of mutual community?

Prayer:

Dear God,
I am convicted of the danger that comes with isolation. I am yielding to the truth that better, more consistent connection with other men will help me make better choices and pursue better priorities. Thank You for the many biblical examples of men who thrived through relationship with others. Give me faith to believe that I have something to give other men as well as glean from them. Please help me overcome my fear of being hurt or misunderstood. Please forgive the ease with which I keep doing my own thing and withhold myself from others.

Guide me as I continue to seek You through the message of this book and grant to me soul-sustaining friendships with other men so that I can increasingly and for Your glory act like the man You have created me to be. In Jesus' name I pray, amen.

NEXT TIME:

HOW PAUL BENEFITED FROM COMMUNITY

36

THE MAN FROM TARSUS

The saying is trustworthy and deserving of full acceptance, that Christ Jesus came into the world to save sinners, of whom I am the foremost.[1]

NOW I AM GOING TO SHOW YOU THAT ONE of the greatest Christians who ever lived, the apostle Paul, was the furthest thing from a loner and loved it that way. It's not about the number of men in your life, but if someone of Paul's quality needed community, who are you and me to insist we don't? If anyone after Jesus Christ knew how to let all you do be done in love, it was the apostle Paul. This man from Tarsus was not some weird, "I wanna talk about my feeeeelllllliiinnngggs," weakling, but he did love people and he wasn't afraid to let them know it. Paul needed and enjoyed others and made sure nobody thought his ministry was a solo. While most of Paul's friends are forgotten to history, he tried hard to let us know his personal community was foundational to his work for Christ:

- Paul opens many of his letters with the names of close friends he was serving with such as Sosthenes in 1 Corinthians, Timothy in 2 Corinthians, Philippians, Colossians, and 1 and 2 Thessalonians along with Silvanus.

- Paul's closest friend, Dr. Luke, stayed with him until he died.[2]
- The Pastoral Epistles were written to protégé pastors Timothy (mentioned 26 times) and Titus (mentioned 13 times).
- Paul acknowledged using an amanuensis such as Tertius in Romans 16:22, who wrote the Epistles as they were dictated.
- Paul wrote Philemon to effect a reconciliation between two of his friends, Philemon and Onesimus.
- Paul closed his letters with personal greetings to recipients and often added the names of those with him from where he writes. For example, Philemon ends with **"Epaphras, my fellow prisoner in Christ Jesus, sends greetings to you, and so do Mark, Aristarchus, Demas, and Luke, my fellow workers."[3]**
- Paul did not just associate with younger men he was training. Acts and the Epistles reveal Paul in relationship with other Christian leaders such as Apollos and Peter and James.
- Not all of Paul's relationships went perfectly. Paul was opposed by men like Alexander and Hymenaeus, and temporarily parted ways with Barnabas and Mark.
- Paul was forsaken by Demas. In the early phases of his second trial in Rome, **"no one came to stand by me, but all deserted me."[4]**
- Paul was also a forgiver and restorer of men, asking, late in life, for Mark and calling him **"useful to me for ministry."[5]**
- Paul referred to friends in very affectionate language.[6] He prayed day and night for them and longed to be reunited with them.
- Scan quickly just a few of Paul's friends not already mentioned: Aristarchus, Gaius, Justus, Marcus, Priscilla, Secundus, Silas, Sopater, Tertius, Trophimus, Tychicus, Andronichus, Apphia, Archippus, Carpus, Epaphroditus, Erastus, Lucius, Lydia, Jason, Junia, Nymphus, Onesiphorus, Phoebe, Tyrannus, and Urba.

I hope this makes the point that Paul's ministry, though itinerant, was filled with meaningful community. These are the people Paul preached with, traveled with, suffered with, endured with, prayed with, laughed and cried with, did life with. Paul was acting like a man, letting all he did be done in love, engaged in community, and enjoying the blessing of biblical friendship.

PAUL ON AN EGO TRIP?

It's getting more and more popular to criticize Paul. I recently read a study of Paul's uses of the personal pronouns in which the author points out the obvious fact that Paul used personal pronouns much more than any other New Testament author. The stats may not be refutable but the reason behind that frequency is what is significant. To explain why Paul mentions himself so often, I need to go back to my own studies.

TALKING ABOUT OURSELVES

When I started out in my doctoral studies, I had no idea how much work was involved in a thesis. My particular school seemed determined to raise the quality of scholarship, and my academic mentor said the requirements were equal to what was asked of his PhD thesis from the University of Michigan. My topic was in the area of self-disclosure of sin among men, so I had to do a lot of work on male behavior characteristics. I had to read a mountain of book chapters and articles and demonstrate proficiency in the reasons men find it so hard to open up about their thoughts and feelings.

You're probably starting to glaze over, so let me cut to the chase on this. Women are hardwired by the Creator to relate, to nurture, and to connect. Men are designed by God to pursue, provide, and protect. Connecting sees relationship as an asset and makes you vulnerable to others. That's why women need protection. Protection sees relationship as a potential threat and makes men aggressive. That's why men need help with connecting. Men are closed and weaker at relationship, favoring protection. Women are open and pursue relationship, requiring protection. Clear? So what do women actually do that makes them so much better at building and sustaining relationship? You know they are doing something in the other room while you and your pals stuff your faces and watch the game, but what? Here it is: they are making themselves known. They are talking to each other about their experiences and being honest about themselves in a way that humans wired for protection, i.e., men, find much more difficult. I will talk in the next study about how we conquer that hurdle as men. For now I simply want to say that the reason Paul had so many friends and was the better for it was because he was a killer in the matter of self-disclosure.

REAL TALK: TELLING IT LIKE IT IS

Men who are cut off, careful, and closed are also lonely and just as vulnerable in a different way as their wives alone in a dark alley after midnight. What makes a man press through his disposition to withhold himself is hardship and heartache. It starts with little things that make life more than you can handle. Next come circumstances that put you on your knees for help you never knew you'd need. Finally something major in health or kids or other essential comes completely unglued, and before you know it the walls are down and you can't play the phony "I have it all together" game anymore.

Before Paul's name was changed, it was Saul. Saul was one of the most hateful, punishing, arrogant, superior guys you would ever want to meet. He had no real friends and his pseudo friends found out they were just cogs in a wheel to accelerate his steamroller. Then one day, when Paul was on a tear to kill Christians in Damascus, Jesus Christ appeared in a burst of light and laid Paul on his face in the mud. Paul was so staggered by the revelation, he wandered blind for a time and struggled to figure it all out.[7] Jesus force-fed Paul the error of everything he had ever done, all that he ever wanted to do or be. Paul was crushed by the revelation of his wicked heart and altered for all time. Pride gone, he referred to himself as the **"chief of sinners."**[8] Superiority gone, he called himself **"the least of the apostles,"**[9] and his mission changed to where **"he who used to persecute us is now preaching the faith he once tried to destroy."**[10]

DISCLOSURE IS THE CURRENCY OF INTIMACY

Men don't open up because they are prideful and self-protective. The lonely, isolated man is that way because he won't make himself known to others. Disclosure of self is the currency of intimacy. It's what our wives want and what true friendship demands. You don't have to spill your guts to everybody or anybody, but God will get you to the place where you know you need to do it with somebody. The temptation to keep it all inside is the downside of being wired as a protector. He loves us too much to leave us alone. You will never fulfill your potential as a man of God going it alone. Check out Paul in Romans 7:18 where he confesses, **"For I know that nothing good dwells in me, that is, in my flesh. For I have the desire to do what is right, but not the ability to carry it out."** In verse 24 he goes so far as to call himself a **"wretched man."** If Paul made that confession in most churches today, the evangelegalists would run him out of the ministry. Paul is so disclosing of his own failings because he is a broken man trying to help other men find what he found in Jesus. Seeing Paul as arrogant because he tells his story is what the arrogant do, but men who have been laid low by Jesus Christ have an awesome story to relay and they don't care if it gets a bit messy.

QUESTIONS FOR REFLECTION

1. Describe your honest reaction to the challenge of greater self-disclosure in your friendships.

2. What do you see as the benefits of "getting real," and what are your fears in doing so?

3. What has happened in your life to move you away from friendship as entertainment and toward friendship as meaningful community?

Prayer:

Dear God,
I come before You, asking for wisdom in applying what I have
just read to my life. Forgive me for wanting to have that kind
of friendship but not always doing what I can to get there.
Give me eyes to see the potential strength and experience
I could offer to the men around me with a truer and more
genuine representation of myself. Deliver me from the fears
and skepticisms I associate with men who open up. Grant that I
will not have to suffer as others have to get past my pride and
sincerely make myself known. Do this for my good and Your
glory. I pray in the name of Your Son, Jesus, amen.

NEXT TIME:
HOW DIVISION PREVENTS COMMUNITY

37

TOGETHER

Do not forsake assembling yourselves together.[1]

IN ONE OF THE SADDEST AND MOST SUBTLE openings to a guy movie, a Medal of Honor–winning Vietnam vet approaches a woman hanging clothes on the line outside a small town in the Pacific Northwest. Inquiring about her son Delmar Berry from his US Army Special Forces unit, he learns his friend died of cancer due to Agent Orange exposure.

Hanging his head and expressing his condolences, John Rambo turns away in great sorrow. While walking into town, Rambo is accosted by a power-hungry local police chief who arrests him for vagrancy and gets him sentenced to thirty-five days in jail. Up to this point, Rambo is quiet but submissive to the escalating abuse, but in the process of choke holding Rambo to dry-shave him, they cause a flashback to his time as a POW, and he goes off on them all. Breaking legs and noses and windows, he escapes to the street, steals a motorcycle, and heads into the mountains.

Filled with rage at this resistance to his authority, the police chief rallies his men to hunt down the fugitive. Using guerrilla tactics and booby traps, Rambo quickly disables the small, disorganized team, severely wounding the deputies and killing their dogs. At dusk, Rambo springs up behind the chief, putting him in a choke hold like the one he broke free from. "I could've killed 'em all; I could've killed you," Rambo says. "In town you're the law, out here it's me! Don't push it! Don't push it or I'll give you a war you won't believe!" Cool scene for sure as Rambo channels his bitterness over the loss of his comrades and betrayal by the country he fought to defend.

Of course, the chief doesn't listen and in the end Rambo kills them all. What is less obvious, if you haven't seen the movie ten plus times like me, is the scene at the end. In an effort to "talk him down," they bring in Rambo's former commander, Colonel Trautman. Some of these lines are too priceless to skip . . .

Chief:	He was just another drifter who broke the law!
Trautman:	Vagrancy, wasn't it? That's gonna look real good on his gravestone in Arlington: Here lies John Rambo, winner of the Congressional Medal of Honor, survivor of countless incursions behind enemy lines. Killed for vagrancy in Jerkwater, USA.
Chief:	Now don't give me any of that c—, Trautman. Do you think Rambo was the only guy who had a tough time in Vietnam? He killed a police officer (expletive).
Trautman:	You're (expletive) lucky he didn't kill all of you. So cool, and . . .
Chief:	Are you tellin' me that two hundred of our men against your boy is a no-win situation for us?
Trautman:	You send that many, don't forget one thing.
Chief:	What?
Trautman:	A good supply of body bags.

When Trautman finally gets through on the radio, Rambo's first words are, "They're all gone sir, every one of them," as he calls out their names. A very touching scene unfolds where Rambo discloses to Trautman the massive wound in his soul, not from the war itself but from the loss of community experienced between men who fought and died side by side. This profound loss is summarized beautifully when Rambo says, "Where is everybody? . . . I . . . I had a friend, . . . What, I had all these guys, man. Back there I had all these guys—who were my friends."

Plain and simple, men need community with other men. Loving, you-before-me, dedicated relationship. If you have never had it, you don't really get it yet, and if you had that community and lost it, you know the cavity it leaves in your soul until you discover it again.

KNOCK OFF THE LIES

As I talk to men all around the world, I discover that they are not much different than we are. They need the same solutions, battle the same things, and believe the same lies. Earlier in this book, we studied the satanic strategy of using lies to disguise, divide, and destroy. Let's focus on the middle word of Satan's plan to defeat you. The word is *divide* and his strategy is to get a wedge between you and men who can support God's work in your life through loving mutual community. As always he does this through lies. See if you recognize any of these common lies men believe that lead them to reject community and live in isolation:

- Nobody understands the struggles I am dealing with.
- I can't trust anyone. Total honesty will be used against me.
- If someone tries to get close to me, they just want something.
- People like me but they don't really know me. I can't risk self-disclosure.
- I've seen Christians kick a guy when he is down. No thanks.
- Christian men are weak, crying, and confessing. Oh please!
- If I really face my secrets, the dam will burst and I will lose it.
- What if I make myself known and the other guys won't reciprocate?

I hear these lies so frequently from the mouths of men that I know they are being implanted there by the **"accuser of our brethren."**[2]

The way to defeat a lie of the Enemy is: name the lie and insert the truth. Jesus did this in Matthew 4 when Satan came to tempt Him after His forty-day fast in the wilderness. Satan urged Him to make stones into bread and Jesus said, **"It is written, 'Man shall not live by bread alone,**

but by every word that comes from the mouth of God.'"[3] This happened two more times, and each time Jesus defeated the lie of the Enemy by quoting from Scripture. Can we afford to do less? What lies do you believe about loving friendship with other men that keep your areas of defeat isolated and unchanged? Take the first lie above: "Nobody understands the struggles I am dealing with." That is clearly untrue because 1 Corinthians 10:13 says, **"No temptation has overtaken you that is not common to man. God is faithful, and he will not let you be tempted beyond your ability, but with the temptation he will also provide the way of escape, that you may be able to endure it."** In every instance we need to name the lie and replace it in our thinking with the truth of God's Word. That's what it means to **"resist the devil, and he will flee from you."**[4]

MY COMMUNITY

For almost fifteen years I met with a group of men every Friday morning at 6 a.m. Each man would report on what he had gleaned from God's Word personally that week and then we would pray for one another. We laughed, we instructed, we carried each other's burdens, and afterward we went out for breakfast. Looking back, I regret ever breaking that pattern. I have found it here and there in other ways, but never as good as that until recently. The reason I withdrew from formal, regular, scheduled community was that I failed to experience the two things my doctoral thesis revealed men absolutely must experience to remain in community. First, men need confidentiality. They have to believe that what they disclose will remain in that room and never be shared with anyone—not a spouse, not a cousin in a far country, no one. Second, men need to experience mutuality. Men need to know that if they bring you in on whatever battles they have kept secret, you won't "leave them hanging," or pridefully conceal the truth about yourself. They need you to quickly match their personal disclosure. **"If we say we have no sin, we deceive ourselves, and the truth is not in us."**[5]

Looking back, I see how I became isolated during the years my kids were in their late teens. I went through a lot of tough stuff, and much of it was worsened because I went through it alone. I allowed the hurt from men I trusted who turned against me to excuse my isolation. I was frustrated that they didn't keep our conversations private and refused to be as open as I was being. I should have helped them change, but I let my disappointment lead me to withdraw, which made things worse. Specific decisions I would never have made in that original community were made with great negative consequences until I forced myself to trust again.

What if you learn from my mistakes and don't let that happen to you? I have just been open here; if we were sitting over coffee, it would be your turn. Don't leave me hanging . . .

QUESTIONS FOR REFLECTION

1. Describe the time in your life when loving community with other men peaked.

2. Which is a bigger issue for you—confidentiality or mutuality?

3. Are there disappointments or hurts that must be forgiven for you to reengage in community?

Prayer:

Father in heaven,
Thank You for the grace of our Lord Jesus Christ that covers us and compels us to extend grace to our brothers. Forgive me for holding others to a standard that I am not living up to and remind me that the standard I use on others will be used on me. I ask You to assault any spirit of independence You see in my life and bring me afresh to full awareness of my need for others. Please keep me from seeing community through the lens of what I need and give me renewed passion to love and serve others as an expression of gratitude for all You have done for

me. Keep my eyes focused on the Lord Jesus, who "came not to be served but to serve, and to give his life as a ransom for many."[6] *In His wonderful name, amen.*

NEXT TIME:

WHAT WE LEARN ABOUT COMMUNITY FROM GOD HIMSELF

38

TRINITY EXPRESSES COMMUNITY

*Lord, you have been our
dwelling place in all generations.*[1]

GOD IS NOT LIKE ANYONE ELSE. We wouldn't know anything about Him unless He chose to reveal Himself to us. And that's exactly what He has done, in more ways than one. Romans 1:20 (NKJV) tells that the existence of God is **"understood by the things that are made."** In fact, our universe in all of its beauty and complexity is shouting, "There's a God, there's a God, there's a God." To deny that reality you have to cover your ears and shut your eyes and sin 'til you drop, a life that Romans 1:18 calls **"suppressing the truth in unrighteousness."** God also wrote a book about Himself, and then He sent His Son to show us as much about Himself as we are ever capable of grasping.

One of the astounding things God has revealed about Himself is that He is Three-in-One, tri-unity, Trinity. This is among the most awesome truths in God's Word. How is it possible that as Jesus was being baptized, the Holy Spirit was **"descending on him like a dove. And a voice came from heaven, 'You are my beloved Son; with you I am well pleased'"**?[2]

Father, Son, and Holy Spirit, eternally existing in three persons, yet one God. How many persons? Three. How many Gods? One! **"Hear, O Israel: The Lord our God, the Lord is one."**[3] Yet Jesus said, **"You know neither me nor my Father. If you knew me, you would know my Father also."**[4]

Jesus is the second person of the Trinity. He is eternal God. If you want to read more on this, Google Jonathan Edwards's unpublished essay on the Holy Spirit in which he argues convincingly and biblically some pretty mind-bending, worship inducing realities. Edwards explains that Jesus Christ is eternally the Father's perfect thoughts about Himself revealed to us in the incarnation. This the Scriptures declare: **"lest the light of the glory of the Gospel of Christ, who is the image of God, should shine on them."**[5] **"Who, being in the form of God."**[6] **"He is the image of the invisible God."**[7] **"He is the radiance of the glory of God and the exact imprint of his nature."**[8] Edwards further argues that the Holy Spirit is the delight that the Father and Son have in this revelation of the divine nature. Take a deep breath. You still with me? I have been meditating on this for months and can't/don't want to get over it. The unceasing fellowship of the Father and Son, their constant communion and immeasurable delight in perfect self-revelation is best summarized by the word *love*, which is the Holy Spirit living within us.

When John writes in 1 John 4:8, 12–13, **"God is love,"** he goes on to say that **"if we love one another, God abides in us and his love is perfected in us. By this we know that we abide in him and he in us, because he has given us of his Spirit."** Paul says in Romans 5:5, **"God's love has been poured into our hearts through the Holy Spirit who has been given to us."** Of course this is a great mystery, and **"now we see in a mirror dimly,"**[9] so don't worry if you can't put all that together perfectly. I have a reason for getting into this.

GOD IS COMMUNITY

Eternal God, existing in three persons: Father, revealing Himself; Son, the revelation of the Father; Holy Spirit, the delight of Father and Son in that revelation best expressed by the word *love*. We are made in God's image; we are made to make ourselves known and delight in the joy of knowing and being known. That loving communion is what God models and we are called to enter into with Him and each other. Nothing matters more to me than leading my family, my wife, my three married kids, and my grandchildren, into that community.

GET A VISION OF GENERATIONAL OBEDIENCE

I am very blessed to come from a long line of Christ-followers on my father's side. In my office I have a photocopy from the inside cover of my great-grandfather Hugh's Bible written almost a hundred years ago:

Hugh MacDonald, born of the flesh May 29, 1875.

Born again of the Spirit through faith in the finished work of the Son, Jesus Christ, January 12, 1917. Romans 5:1, **"Therefore, since we have been justified by faith, we have peace with God through our Lord Jesus Christ."**

Hugh, a Holstein cattle farmer, was forty-two when he gave his life to Christ. By this time his four sons were already grown. Jack, my grandfather, chose to follow the example of his dad, Hugh, and embraced the Savior too. Hugh's other three sons, Donald, Dugal, and Bruce, all vocally and decidedly rejected Jesus Christ. One adult son embraced the Savior; three did not. In fact, my great-uncle Donald just died in 2007. He was ninety-seven years old. My dad went and visited him in his last weeks of his life. He wanted nothing to do with Christ and at this moment is sadly experiencing the consequences of rejecting the Savior.

I could fill a separate book with the stories of heartache that accompanied my great-uncles' decisions not to believe, not to follow Jesus Christ. What if my grandfather had sided with his brothers' profanity and not his father's faith? My great-grandfather Hugh bowed to Jesus Christ when most around him did not. My grandfather Jack chose Jesus even though his brothers did not. My father, Verne, chose to follow Jesus while some of his siblings did not. Through me to my two sons and son-in-law as well as five grandsons, (so far) this chain of obedience to Christ can stretch six generations. Nothing is more important to me than that. Nothing should be more important to you than generational obedience as the legacy of your life. How can we even consider the possibility of someone in our family not joining us in the eternal communion and endless joy with the triune God in heaven?

A CHAIN IN THE PULPIT

At our Act Like Men conferences, Mark Driscoll takes a thick, heavy chain into the pulpit and preaches a message on the genealogy in Genesis. In one of the more powerful sermons for men I have ever heard, he challenges men to recognize where they are in the chain. Mark is a "first link," saved from a home with an alcoholic abusive father. In God's grace Mark's dad has also trusted Christ, adding a link to the chain on the front end. The point is to find yourself on that chain. I am a fourth link and realize that **"to whom much is given, from him much will be required."**[10] Just this week my oldest son Luke's wife, Kristen, texted the following about their second son: "Reid accepted Jesus tonight on his way home from church." It's happening. My father's great-grandsons believing on Christ for salvation. I pray frequently to live long enough to see one of my grandsons preach the gospel as my father has heard several of his.

Figure out where you are on the chain and start giving yourself through prayer and action to seeing this awesome vision become a reality. Recognize that an isolated life, with little connection to other men, is the exact opposite of the man who will see the salvation of subsequent generations as his legacy. Life is about reaching people with the message of the cross for the glory of God. Any other life purpose not toward that end is an illusionary deception installed by the Evil One to push your family tree into the abyss.

ARE YOU WITH ME?

You see what I am doing here, don't you? I am trying to convince you that men need friendships with other men. I am trying to persuade you to include community in your determination to act like a man. So far, I have shown the call to love in our theme verse, connected that priority to the context men tend to avoid—friendship with other men. Next we saw many biblical examples of how community between men is blessed and its absence has grave consequences. Then we learned that one of the greatest Christians who ever lived, the apostle Paul, was deeply involved in life-giving, faith-sustaining community with other men and that his frequent self-disclosure that men find so tough began when Paul was taken down hard by Jesus Christ and "tapped out" to His lordship.

Now I am declaring that far from an optional leisure activity, loving mutual community is at the core of the Godhead and what you are created for, saved for, and invited into. I am saying that avoiding community with other Christian men while praying that your family will find it is basically hypocritical, right? Sadly, I know that if you resist God's call to community, He has some tough stuff planned to get you over the hump.

QUESTIONS FOR REFLECTION

1. Write out your thoughts about this teaching on community within the Godhead.

2. If heaven is the ultimate and eternal communion of the saints with each other and God, how should that affect our view of community today?

3. When was a time you felt most joy in knowing and being known by a friend?

Prayer:

Oh Triune God,
My thoughts of You are such a trifle compared to Your infinite, eternal perfections. I worship You in spirit and truth, I bow before You in silence and awe. How awesome is Your name. You have set Your glory above the heavens and ignited a passion in my heart to live for Your glory. I ask You to penetrate my heart

*with the priority of expressing Your loving nature by the way
I give myself in relationship to others. Please allow Your great
love, demonstrated through Christ, and living in me by the
Holy Spirit to be poured out to everyone I meet today. In Jesus'
precious name, amen.*

NEXT TIME:

JESUS LAYS DOWN THE LAW ABOUT LOVE

UNDER ORDERS TO LOVE

*A new commandment I give to you, that
you love one another: just as I have loved you,
you also are to love one another.*[1]

THIS, THE SECOND TO THE LAST of our studies, is going to be quite personal, as I try to reflect the kind of vulnerability Jesus personified, and the kind you will need as you grow in letting **"all that you do be done in love."**[2] At the age of twenty-seven, my wife and I were just finishing seminary five hundred miles from where we grew up, but with the nations on our heart. I had been studying churches in North America and realized that very few really impacted the world. At that time 80–85 percent of all churches in North America had plateaued or were in decline. Only one in ten pastors starting out in ministry were making it to retirement still vocationally serving a local church. The average length of any single pastorate was less than four years, yet a study by the Southern Baptist Convention revealed that churches with high pastoral turnover were ineffective in reaching people with the gospel. Our passion to "stay put" grew from these grim statistics and shaped our praying as graduation got close. "God, we will go anywhere You want us to go, but let us stay there." However, it wasn't just a statistical thing.

ENDURING COMMUNITY

When you begin to understand that joyful, mutual, loving community is the central celebration within the Godhead. When you begin to comprehend that we are invited to share that fellowship through faith in the finished work of Christ. When you embrace the certainty that we are heading now toward a blissful participation in soul-satisfying community that will never end. If you can imagine for a moment what it will mean to enjoy relationship without ego, or hurt, or fear, or conflict, all of us moving forward together to the melody of God Himself in a perfect harmony to a galactic choreography that staggers the mind. When you finally see and accept that heavenly trajectory for the family of God, you know you have to give yourself to it here on earth.

Now in my fifties, I am able to articulate the priority of community a lot better than I could in my twenties, but I knew then and still believe that church is the laboratory and practice session for the great community experience ahead. Why do most pastors move from church to church? The reason is simple: depravity. It's that twisted "me before you" opposite of love inclination that plagues each one of us.

The initial phase with the "new pastor" is frequently called the "honeymoon." During this time he and the congregation are celebrating mutual strengths, but that stage typically doesn't last. Over time, disappointments come, deficiencies are observed, rose-colored glasses are put away, and before too long, "God is calling" the pastor to move on. Off he goes with his drawerful of sermons, avoiding what God is teaching him and allowing a congregation to do the same. The alternative, of course, is the most difficult obedience God asks from His children: forgiveness. When we see the faults of others, we are to forgive and forbear in humility. We are commanded, **"Let each esteem others better than himself."**[3] Our Lord was not simply making suggestions when He said, **"You hypocrite, first take the log out of your own eye, and then you will see clearly to take the speck out of your brother's eye."**[4]

When will we see that the depravity of the human heart is *not* most clearly on display in the gay pride parade or at the abortion clinic? The greatest failures in human experience are not seen in the activist atheist rallying unbelief or the scorning skeptic ridiculing Jesus Christ, or the senseless wars, or baffling famines. The greatest failure in human existence is the failure of Christ-followers to **"love one another earnestly from a pure heart"**[5] and to heed the words of Christ: **"By this all people will know that you are my disciples, if you have love for one another."**[6]

The gospel's first failure is not lack of proclamation but lack of application. Churches closing at a rate of six thousand per year in North America are not doing so because of worship style or form of government or methodology. They are failing because regardless of your preference on those points, it's pointless to deny the true cause behind debates and divisions—a failure to love. Pastors are not falling and failing at epidemic rates because of a lack of commitment to truth or because they don't know how to comfort the grieving; our failure is the same as the failure of our people—it's a failure to love.

IT ALL COMES DOWN TO THIS

Given the impossibility of *not* failing one another, when the Bible says, **"We all stumble in many ways,"**[7] the only way forward in loving community with one another is forgiveness. I was pretty young when I first voiced the words, "There are no enduring relationships without forgiveness." Through the years I have kept believing and struggled to practice that powerful maxim. In our homes, where we work, in our friendships, we come inevitably to a fork in the road where we must decide, "Will I forgive that?" If the answer is yes, we go forward together in love. If we choose "no, I will not forgive," at that point we will tend to amplify the fault we observe to excuse our withdrawal into bitterness. Everyone loses—and the gospel most of all.

THE COST OF LOVE AND FORGIVENESS

A true commitment to enduring relationships has been the crucible of my sanctification. I began as a "truth guy" proclaiming God's standard and calling people to holiness. I was afraid of nothing. Preaching the authority of God's Word without apology was my passion. That conviction remains strong, but the tone and emphasis has shifted dramatically even these last five years. I have pastored the same church my wife and I planted after seminary for twenty-six years and counting. During that time there have been several partings of the way with key leaders.

In every instance, I located a specific shortcoming of my own that seemed to precipitate or at least enflame the situation and I went to work on that. "I need to be more forthright; I need to deal with problem people sooner; I need to make better hiring decisions and stop trying to control people; I need to be less demanding; and more compassionate," etc. Looking back now, I see my participation in every one of those situations as a failure to love. Yes, I took a stand and stood up to people who were stepping all over the church and me. Yes, I refused to put off difficult decisions, eliminated conflicts of interest, and refused to be a "respecter of persons." What I significantly failed to do was **let all that you do be done in love.** I had to learn, "If you are wrong in the way you are right, you are wrong even if you are right." Pain is an effective instructor.

REAPING AND SOWING

Early in 2009, as I went through cancer treatment and saw my mother begin her descent down a road of great suffering toward her death from ALS, I was privately seeking the Lord for a deep transformation in my own life and ministry. I recognized that I needed to accelerate my growth in grace and mentioned it frequently in sermons at that time. As I wrestled with my love deficiencies and the impact it was having on my ministry, I was also engaged in ministry associations with other pastors and saw, as in a mirror, how a lot of "truth" guys were weak in loving relational harmony. One example that stands out is a conference some of us did together. The idea was to get professing Christian leaders in the room who are known to differ greatly on theology or methodology and just talk with each other. The goal was not to correct or instruct each other but to listen. We had no intention of confronting the other guys. The goal was simply to model loving interaction about significant issues. It was a worthy goal to be sure, but even more, in the end, a confirmation of our collective deficiency in love.

The conference brought a deluge of censure: you weren't strong enough, you compromised the truth, you can't associate with men like *that* or you agree with them. That line of thinking grew into a tsunami of criticism toward me personally and almost everything I had ever done. Looking back it seems the Lord was saying, "Instead of holding a conference on public displays of love, why don't we put you through the gauntlet personally and teach you how to love." Ouch!

It was a painful season to be sure, but a truly refining one. Jesus Christ kept loving His friends, loved even His enemies, and **"when he was reviled he did not revile in return; . . . but continued entrusting himself to him who judges justly."**[8] I am still not doing that perfectly, but by God's grace I am doing it increasingly. What's your story of growing in love?

QUESTIONS FOR REFLECTION

1. In what ways has your life shown the effects of love deficiency?

2. Who is most in need of God's love expressed through you today and what will you do about that?

3. Will you take some extra time and journal something similar to what you have just read? Call it My Journey toward Love. Be as honest and open as you can, and choose a friend to share your story with.

Prayer:

Dear Father God,
Perfect in love so wonderfully expressed in Your Son, Jesus Christ. Thank You for calling me to this highest expression of who You are. Thank You for saving me to a future where we will

know and love perfectly. I submit afresh to Your desire to grow me in love now. Give me fresh eyes to see the people around me, those I need to forgive, those I need to forbear with, and those I need to leave in Your hands and wait with open arms for the day of reconciliation. Thank You for Your patience with my sinful selfishness that harms Your kingdom and wounds Your people. Grow me in the matchless love of my Savior, Jesus Christ. In His name I pray, amen.

NEXT TIME:
THE HOLY SPIRIT'S HELP WITH COMMUNITY

40

STRENGTH TO LOVE

*Therefore, as you received Christ Jesus the
Lord, so walk in him, rooted and built up
in him and established in the faith, just as
you were taught, abounding in thanksgiving.*[1]

I LOVE TO TAKE MY GRANDKIDS TO THE CIRCUS, best of all
Cirque du Soleil, which combines all the ancient arts of acrobatics in contexts of modern artistry. Most remarkable to me is not the trapeze or the high wire or stacking of people one on top of the other. I am most amazed, always have been, by the jugglers.

Anthony Gatto is the greatest juggler of all time. A Floridian by birth, he was astounding audiences by the age of five and holds eleven world records, starring for years in Cirque du Soleil. His records are for keeping specific objects aloft for longer times and in greater numbers than anyone else. Eleven rings, nine balls, eight clubs. To put that in perspective, only Gatto can juggle eight clubs because they are so big and awkward. Of the maybe a hundred people in the world who can juggle seven clubs, a few seconds would be maximum, but Gatto can do that for four minutes.

What's mind-boggling is that Gatto, the world's best, decided to stop juggling professionally altogether and no one is sure why, because he won't talk about it. From YouTube videos where he sets world records in a cold sweat to actual performances where thousands of throws, sometimes four per second, are executed every time with pinpoint accuracy, Gatto seems tireless. But he wasn't. He quit. I think he quit because juggling is exhausting.[2]

THE BEST FOR LAST

This is the final study and I'm not gonna phone it in. Careful application of what follows is essential to success in the five imperatives of Act Like Men. In fact, what I will share here is the single greatest insight I have to living the Christian life effectively and it starts with your retirement as a juggler. Do you know what I mean?

Juggling is exhausting, very much like the Christian life most men are living. Be strong, stay focused, love Jesus, walk the dog, lead your family, put the kids to bed, bring home the bacon, listen to your wife, solve problems, live with passion, connect with other men, serve the church . . . and then crash and the circus music halts! Hear me; it is absolutely not possible to keep all those things in the air. And because it hurts to have stuff you care about crash at your feet, most men opt for one of two things: either pretend you're juggling all that stuff when you know you aren't, or stop caring about the juggle altogether and spend your energies on something actually doable. Men are checking out at prolific rates because any casual review of the "Christian Man" job description has at the top "Impossible!"

GET THIS AND GET EVERYTHING

I was in my late thirties before this truth took an exhausted pastor of fifteen years and gave him a sustainable trajectory. Has anyone ever explained to you that Christ has made no provision for you—on your own—to live the Christian life? The Christian life is not nor was it ever intended to be you as a professional juggler of the latest list of biblical priorities. That is not what this book is and I know that's not possible. We have no more ability to sanctify (change) ourselves than we had ability to save ourselves.

Colossians 2:6 makes this clear: **"As you received Christ Jesus the**

Lord, so walk in him." Are you doing that? To be saved you had to admit to God your complete inability to save yourself. **"For by grace you have been saved, through faith. And this is not of your own doing; it is the gift of God, not a result of works, so that no one may boast."**[3] You're probably saying, "I get it, you can't save yourself, I've known that a long time, move on." Yes let's: **"As you received Jesus Christ the Lord,** *so walk in him."* Do you get it? You have no ability to live the Christian life, no more capacity in yourself to live the gospel than you had to believe the gospel in the first place.

BAD PREACHING BY ME

Just yesterday a man in our church, a wonderful servant of Jesus, dropped dead of a heart attack. When I finish this chapter, I am going to his house to pray with his heartbroken wife and three daughters. I might read to them from a passage I preached poorly for many years. Second Corinthians 4:8–9 says, **"We are afflicted in every way, but not crushed; perplexed, but not driven to despair; persecuted, but not forsaken; struck down, but not destroyed."** I stood behind a pulpit and tried to inspire folks to believe those promises but somehow, incredibly, stopped short of the part that brings it home. I was like a man talking to starving people about food but not telling them where to find it. How could I have been so blind not to see verse 10? **"Always carrying in the body the death of Jesus,** *so that the life of Jesus may also be manifested in our bodies."*[4]

The Christian life is the life of Jesus in me by the Holy Spirit. Christianity is not me striving to live like Jesus as a "thank-you" for saving me. Christianity is Christ taking up residence in me by the Holy Spirit and living His resurrection life through me.

IT'S EVERYWHERE

The Bible is a unified whole ultimately authored by God Himself, so once your eyes are opened to the truth that Jesus lives the Christian life, not you, you begin to see it everywhere. Galatians 2:20 says it well. **"I**

have been crucified with Christ. It is no longer I who lives, but Christ who lives in me."[5] When you received Jesus Christ as your Savior, He came to live within you by His Holy Spirit, and that is the *life* of the Christian life. Jesus will not wrestle or fight with you; as long as your flesh wants to be in control, it will be. I love Romans 5:10: **"For if while we were enemies we were reconciled to God by the death of his Son, much more, now that we are reconciled, shall we be saved by his life."** *Salvation* is a big Bible word that can mean anything from election to conversion, to sanctification, and even to our ultimate glorification in heaven. Context determines whether it means a part or the whole. In Romans 5:10 Paul is saying that conversion, or reconciliation, was accomplished by the death of Jesus, so that sanctification, the Christian life between initial faith and heaven, can be accomplished by His life. Saved by His life.

A turning point for me came when I read a little book I now give out to people every chance I get, by a wonderful man named Ian Thomas. It's called *The Saving Life of Christ*. Pick it up if you want to go much deeper into this subject than we can here.

STOP JUGGLING AND START COMMUNING

As kids we used to sing a chorus in vacation Bible school from 1 Thessalonians 5, which contains a pretty exhausting list of dos and don'ts for Christians: **"Rejoice always, pray without ceasing, give thanks in all circumstances. . . . Do not quench the Spirit. Do not despise prophecies, but test everything; hold fast what is good. Abstain from every form of evil"** (vv. 16–22). By the time you get to the end of the list, that's a lot of balls to have in the air. Working up a sweat, juggling with all your might, but knowing you can't keep it up forever, is no way to live the Christian life. Worse, it's a slap in the face to Jesus Christ who not only died for our sin but rose from the dead to live His life through us. How much we would glean if we would get past the list to the power God provided to get it done. First Thessalonians doesn't stop with the list, even though that annoying kids' chorus did. The passage ends with the most important part: **"He who calls you is faithful;** *He will surely do* *it.*"[6] How do we miss this? Paul isn't changing the subject; he's finishing the thought! God doesn't just call me to do it; He Himself is the doer, if I will just lean into my constant communion with Him and yield my **"members as instruments of righteousness."**[7]

As you study the New Testament with this truth in mind, it will amaze you how many descriptions of what Christians are supposed to be doing are followed up or preceded by that warning, a sort of "now kids, don't try this at home." Those are the Holy Spirit's warnings to remind us where the strength comes for obedience. That's the exchanged life—where we allow Christ to live His life through us. Other Bible verses you can study describing the exchanged, Holy Spirit–empowered life of love include John 15:1–5; Romans 5:10; 6:5; 8:10; 2 Corinthians 2:14; 4:10; Philippians 4:19; Colossians 1:27; 2:6; 3:3.

QUESTIONS FOR REFLECTION

1. Describe your own experience with "juggling," and what it's like when things crash.

2. What word most fairly summarizes your Christian life: exhausted, defeated, or empowered? And why? Where have you known victory you would attribute to the Holy Spirit living the life of Christ through you?

3. In what ways has this study most impacted your life, and what do you believe God is leading you to do in response?

Prayer:

Heavenly Father,
Forgive me for resorting to my own strength, which is helpless when You have offered me Your abundant, inexhaustible strength to face whatever You have allowed into my life. I so long to gain and maintain clarity on this point of empowering

community with You as the foundation of all that I am and do. I can do all things through Christ who strengthens me; I can do nothing of eternal value in my own strength. You have given me Your Holy Spirit, as the power to live in community with others and love them as You would. I so want to live in the power of Your Spirit, setting aside more and more evidences of the exhausting life that tempts me every day. I'm relying on Your Spirit to issue piercing warnings each time I stray into that danger zone. Please get glory for Your name as You empower me to act like a man and lead other men in this worthy calling. In Jesus' name I pray, amen.

SUBJECTS

BE WATCHFUL

SUBJECTS	ACT LIKE MEN	BE WATCHFUL
TEXT FOCUS	#1 Act Like Men	#9 Be Watchful
SUMMARY WORD	#2 Quality	#10 Urgency
O.T. FAILURE	#3 Eli	#11 Esau
PAUL'S EXAMPLE	#4 Repentance	#12 Rough Edges
SATAN'S LIE	#5 Good Enough	#13 Angel Of Light
FATHER PERFECTS	#6 Quality Control	#14 Promises
SON PERSONIFIES	#7 Quality Example	#15 Focused
HOLY SPIRIT EMPOWERS	#8 Enables Quality	#16 Discipline

#17
Stand Firm
In The Faith

#18
Clarity

#19
Solomon

#20
Kept The Faith

#21
Excuses Work

#22
Sovereignty

#23
Clear Example

#24
Alarm

#25
Be Strong

#26
Authenticity

#27
Samson

#28
Suffering

#29
Promoting
Slippage

#30
Confronting
David

#31
Repentance

#32
Convicting

#33
Do Every
Thing In Love

#34
Community

#35
Isolation

#36
Self-Disclosure

#37
Divide

#38
Trinity Pictures
Community

#39
Forgiveness

#40
His Life, Our Life

NOTES

STUDY 1: *Acting Like Men*

1. 1 Corinthians 16:13–14
2. Hebrews 4:12
3. S. J. Kistemaker and W. Hendricksen, New Testament Commentary, vol. 18, *Exposition of the First Epistle to the Corinthians* (Grand Rapids: Baker, 1993).
4. Genesis 2:18
5. Genesis 2:18
6. Proverbs 20:3
7. James 3:2

STUDY 2: *A Quality Man*

1. Proverbs 9:9
2. Romans 7:15
3. 2 Timothy 1:7
4. James 1:20

STUDY 3: *Not a Quality Man*

1. Proverbs 22:1
2. Genesis 6:3 NKJV
3. 1 Samuel 2:16
4. 1 Samuel 2:17
5. 1 Samuel 2:24
6. 1 Samuel 3:13
7. 1 Samuel 2:25
8. 1 Samuel 2:29–30

STUDY 4: *And the Gold Goes to . . .*

1. 1 Corinthians 9:24
2. Jeremiah 17:9
3. Ezekiel 18:30
4. Mark 1:15
5. See for example 2 Corinthians 7:9–10
6. Philippians 3:4
7. 1 John 1:8
8. 1 Timothy 1:15

STUDY 5: *"What Are You Looking At?"*

1. Proverbs 3:7 NKJV
2. Matthew 4:1; Luke 11:19; Revelation 12:9–10; Luke 10:18; 2 John 7; John 8:44; 2 Corinthians 11:14
3. John 9:5
4. John 3:19 NKJV
5. Romans 14:12
6. 1 Peter 1:16

STUDY 6: *Truly—As Good as It Gets*

1. Deuteronomy 32
2. Charles Hodge, *Theology Proper,* http://www.monergism.com/thethreshold/sdg/theologyproper.html#n02).
3. Genesis 1:4, 10, 12, 18, 21, 25, 31

STUDY 7: *Disneyland Quality*

1. Colossians 1:19–20
2. Song of Solomon 2:15
3. James 1:8
4. Exodus 34:6–7
5. Matthew 16:26
6. Mark 1:35
7. James 1:20
8. Matthew 13:58
9. 1 Timothy 5:24
10. Matthew 15:8; Isaiah 29:13

STUDY 8: *Let Your Partner Take the Lead*

1. Romans 8:14
2. See Romans 10:17

STUDY 9: *Keep Your Head Up*

1. Matthew 24:43
2. Nehemiah 4:9
3. Nehemiah 12:25

STUDY 10: *Snap Out of It!*

1. 1 Timothy 5:8
2. Luke 10:27
3. Mark 8:36 NKJV
4. Lyle Dorsett, *A Passion for God* (Chicago: Moody Publishers, 2008), 160.
5. Ibid., 81.
6. Ibid., 106.
7. Ecclesiastes 9:10

STUDY 11: *Man—Do I Feel Stupid!*

1. 1 Timothy 4:16 ESV and NKJV combined
2. Malachi 1:2–3
3. Hebrews 12:16
4. Hebrews 12:17
5. Philippians 2:12
6. 1 Timothy 4:16 ESV and NKJV combined

STUDY 12: *You're Only Lying to Yourself*

1. Philippians 2:3
2. 1 John 4:20
3. 1 Corinthians 1:27
4. 1 Timothy 3:2; Titus 1:6
5. Proverbs 3:7
6. Philippians 2:3
7. James 2:13

STUDY 13: *Headed for the Ditch on a Sunny Day*

1. John 10:10
2. 2 Corinthians 11:14
3. John 8:44
4. C. S. Lewis, *Screwtape Letters* (New York: HarperCollins, 2001), 123.
5. Acts 20:28 NIV

STUDY 14: *Never Give Up*

1. Psalm 116:1–2
2. 2 Peter 3:9 NKJV
3. Acts 16:31 NKJV, italics added
4. Jeremiah 1:12
5. Luke 18:1
6. Psalm 116:1–2
7. See James 4:2.

STUDY 15: *Jesus Was Fired Up*

1. John 2:17
2. Matthew 6:10
3. Colossians 1:16
4. John 1:14
5. Colossians 1:20
6. John 2:13–17
7. John 8:1–11
8. Mark 6:45–52
9. Matthew 23:33–35
10. John 18:3

STUDY 16: *Watchful Home Improvement*

1. Proverbs 9:10
2. Proverbs 29:19

STUDY 17: *Urgently Unclear*

1. 1 Corinthians 16:13
2. Proverbs 29:22
3. 2 Timothy 4:7, italics added
4. 2 Timothy 1:14
5. Jude 3, italics added

STUDY 18: *A Craving for Clarity*

1. Jeremiah 15:16
2. Sebastian Klein, "The Secret to Career Contentment: Don't Follow Your Passion," in *Fast Company* magazine, online, February 12, 2014.
3. 2 Corinthians 13:5
4. John 14:16–17. Ephesians 4:1–7 also lays out seven essential "ones" of the faith, beginning with God.

5. Romans 3:23; 6:23. Also see Psalm 51:5.
6. Colossians 2:13–14
7. Acts 16:31
8. John 3:16; 10:10

STUDY 19: *Clarity in Crisis*

1. Ecclesiastes 12:13
2. Romans 6:11 NKJV
3. Colossians 3:2
4. Ecclesiastes 1:15. Ecclesiastes 1:2
5. Ecclesiastes 1:3
6. Ecclesiastes 1:4
7. See also Ecclesiastes 3:11

STUDY 20: *Paul's Clarity*

1. Philippians 3:13–14
2. 1 Timothy 1:20
3. Acts 14:19
4. 2 Corinthians 11:24
5. Acts 16:16-24
6. 2 Corinthians 11:25
7. 2 Timothy 4:10
8. 2 Timothy 4:7
9. 1 Corinthians 11:1
10. Proverbs 29:25

STUDY 21: *Clarity in Conflict*

1. 1 Samuel 15:22
2. 1 Samuel 10–30 tells the tragic unraveling of a leader's life.
3. 1 Samuel 13:8–14
4. 1 Samuel 14:24–46
5. 1 Samuel 15:1–9
6. 1 Samuel 15:22
7. Matthew 8:13
8. Philippians 2:13

STUDY 22: *Clarity—The Father Personifies It*

1. Isaiah 6:1
2. Revelation 20:11, 12, 15
3. Ezekiel 1:28
4. 1 Timothy 6:16

5. Exodus 33:20 NASB
6. Isaiah 6:1
7. Isaiah 6:3
8. Leviticus 11:44; 1 Peter 1:16
9. 1 Corinthians 15:58
10. Joshua 24:15
11. 1 Kings 18:21
12. 1 Corinthians 16:13
13. Ephesians 4:1

STUDY 23: *The Clarity of Christ*

1. John 6:38
2. John 2:4; Matthew 26:45; John 12:23
3. Track His interactions with Jewish leaders in Mark 11:27– 12:34.
4. Matthew 9:36
5. Luke 2:49
6. John 10:10; John 8:32
7. Luke 14:26
8. Luke 9:62
9. Matthew 6:33
10. Luke 10:27
11. John 8:24
12. John 10:30
13. John 14:9

STUDY 24: *This Is Not a Test*

1. Galatians 5:16
2. 1 Peter 5:8
3. John 15:5
4. Oswald Sanders, *The Holy Spirit and His Gifts* (Grand Rapids: Zondervan, 1970), 92.

STUDY 25: *The Battle to Be Strong*

1. 1 Corinthians 16:13
2. Ephesians 6:10
3. 2 Timothy 2:1 NKJV
4. Matthew 5: 29–30
5. Matthew 5:29
6. 2 Corinthians 5:17, author translation
7. Matthew 7:22–23
8. 2 Timothy 2:22 NASB

STUDY 26: *The Strength of Authenticity*

1. Mark 3:25
2. Matthew 7:27
3. See Numbers 11:20
4. Hebrews 13:4

STUDY 27: *The Samson Syndrome*

1. Judges 16:20
2. Judges 16:5
3. Judges 16:20
4. Proverbs 9:10
5. Judges 14:1–2
6. Judges 14:2
7. Judges 14:3
8. 1 Timothy 1:19
9. Judges 16:6

STUDY 28: *The Thorny Way*

1. 2 Corinthians 12:9
2. 1 Corinthians 9:27
3. 2 Corinthians 11:28
4. 1 Corinthians 2:3
5. 2 Corinthians 12:20
6. Ephesians 6:19–20
7. Romans 8:28
8. 2 Corinthians 12:9
9. 2 Corinthians 12:9
10. 2 Corinthians 12:9, author translation
11. 2 Corinthians 12:10

STUDY 29: *Before the Fall*

1. Numbers 32:23
2. 1 Samuel 13:14
3. John 4:4 NASB

STUDY 30: *Our Strong God*

1. Psalm 51:6 HCSB
2. James 1:17
3. Psalm 51:6 HCSB

STUDY 31: *Back to Repentance*

1. 2 Corinthians 7:10

2. Romans 11:33 NKJV
3. See Isaiah 40:28–29
4. John 10:18 NKJV
5. 1 John 1:9
6. Matthew 3:2
7. Matthew 4:17

STUDY 32: *Letting Your Partner Lead*

1. Romans 8:14
2. Romans 8:14 NKJV

STUDY 33: *Doing It All in Love?*

1. Romans 12:9 NKJV
2. 1 Corinthians 16:14
3. See Romans 13:10; Galatians 5:14
4. 2 Timothy 3:16, author translation
5. 2 Peter 1:21 NKJV
6. 1 Corinthians 16:14

STUDY 34: *Love Has a Lot to Do with It*

1. John 15:13
2. 1 Corinthians 16:14
3. Ephesians 4:15
4. 1 Corinthians 13:8 NKJV
5. John 15:13, italics added
6. 1 John 4:20
7. Jerry Cook and Stanley C. Baldwin, *Love, Acceptance and Forgiveness* (Ventura, CA: Regal Books; rev. ed. [July 15, 2009]), 14–15.
8. Ephesians 4:25

STUDY 35: *Two or More Are More*

1. Ecclesiastes 4:12
2. James 1:23–24
3. 1 Samuel 24:3
4. Jonah 4:3
5. Judges 14–16
6. 1 Kings 18–19
7. Job 16:2
8. 1 Samuel 31
9. Jonah 4:3, 8
10. Jonah 4:4, 9

11. Jonah 4:19
12. Judges 14:3
13. Judges 14:11
14. 1 Kings 19:4
15. 1 Kings 19:4
16. 1 Kings 19:8
17. 1 Kings 19:9
18. Job 1:8
19. Job 2:9
20. Job 16:2
21. 1 Corinthians 16:14
22. Daniel 3:17–18
23. Numbers 14:6–9
24. Genesis 13:1; 14:16
25. Exodus 5:1
26. Exodus 18:7, 24
27. 1 Samuel 18:1; 20:17

STUDY 36: *The Man from Tarsus*

1. 1 Timothy 1:15
2. 2 Timothy 4:11
3. Philemon 23–24
4. 2 Timothy 4:16
5. 2 Timothy 4:11
6. Philippians 4:1; 1 Thessalonians 2:20
7. Acts 9:1–31
8. 1 Timothy 1:15 NKJV
9. 1 Corinthians 15:9
10. Galatians 1:23

STUDY 37: *Together*

1. Hebrews 10:25, author translation
2. Revelation 12:10 NKJV
3. Matthew 4:4
4. James 4:7

5. 1 John 1:8
6. Mark 10:45

STUDY 38: *Trinity Expresses Community*

1. Psalm 90:1
2. Mark 1:11
3. Mark 12:29
4. John 8:19
5. 2 Corinthians 4:4
6. Philippians 2:6
7. Colossians 1:15
8. Hebrews 1:3
9. 1 Corinthians 13:12
10. Luke 12:48

STUDY 39: *Under Orders to Love*

1. John 13:34
2. 1 Corinthians 16:14
3. Philippians 2:3 NKJV
4. Matthew 7:5
5. 1 Peter 1:22
6. John 13:35
7. James 3:2
8. 1 Peter 2:23

STUDY 40: *Strength to Love*

1. Colossians 2:6–7
2. Adapted from an article at Grantland.com by Jason Fagone, March 18, 2014.
3. Ephesians 2:8–9
4. Italics added
5. Italics added
6. 1 Thessalonians 5:24
7. Romans 6:13

IT'S TIME TO
ACT LIKE MEN

The Act Like Men Conference is a hard-hitting two-day event designed to challenge men with the truths from 1 Corinthians 16:13-14. No excuses, just get here.

ACTLIKEMEN.COM | ***888.581.9673***

ACT LIKE MEN CONFERENCE

TOP 10 MESSAGES FOR MEN

Get the *Top 10 Messages for Men* that tackle the tough issues men deal with today. Find these resources and more at ACTLIKEMEN.COM.